Eyewitness
ASTRONOMY

Calculator
(19th century)

Model of Stonehenge

An ornamental
cosmotherium
(19th century)

Japanese sundial
(19th century)

Cosmosphere,
depicting the celestial
sphere (19th century)

HISTORIÆ COELESTIS
LIBRI PRIMI,
PARS SEPTIMA.
OBSERVATIONES
Altitudinum & Distantiarum
SOLIS à VERTICE
QUADRANTIBUS,
NECNON ET
VENERIS à SOLE DISTANTIAS SEXTANTE,
Refractionem Coelestium Montium Investigandi gratia,
GRENOVICI
In Observatorio Regio,
CAPTAS
COMPREHENDENS.

The star catalogue of John Flamsteed (1725)

Napier's bones

Prisms used in a
19th-century spectroscope

Eyewitness
ASTRONOMY

Written by
KRISTEN LIPPINCOTT

Refracting telescope
(19th century)

Andromeda galaxy

Persian astrolabe
(18th century)

DK Publishing, Inc.

Bust of Galileo

Beam balance to find mass

Printed constellation card
(19th century)

Micrometer for use with
a telescope

19th-century orrery
showing Uranus with
its four known satellites

DK

LONDON, NEW YORK, MELBOURNE,
MUNICH, and DELHI

Project editor Charyn Jones
Art editor Ron Stobbart
Design assistant Elaine C Monaghan
Production Meryl Silbert
Picture research Becky Halls, Deborah Pownall
Managing editor Josephine Buchanan
Managing art editor Lynne Brown
Special photography Tina Chambers, Clive Streeter
Editorial consultant Dr. Heather Couper

REVISED EDITION
Managing editor Linda Esposito
Senior editor Shaila Awan
Managing art editor Jane Thomas
Category publisher Linda Martin
Art director Simon Webb
Editor and reference compiler Clare Hibbert
Art editor Rebecca Johns
Consultant Robin Scagell
Production Jenny Jacoby
Picture research Bridget Tily
DTP designer Siu Yin Ho

U.S. editor Elizabeth Hester
Senior editor Beth Sutinis
Art director Dirk Kaufman
U.S. DTP designer Milos Orlovic
U.S. production Chris Avgherinos

This Eyewitness ® Guide has been conceived by
Dorling Kindersley Limited and Editions Gallimard

This edition first published in the United States in 2004
by DK Publishing, Inc., 375 Hudson Street, New York, NY 10014

04 05 06 07 08 10 9 8 7 6 5 4 3 2 1

A catalog record for this book is
available from the Library of Congress.

ISBN 0-7566-0656-X (HC) 0-7566-0655-1 (Library Binding)

Color reproduction by
Colourscan, Singapore
Printed in China by Toppan Printing Co., (Shenzhen) Ltd.

Discover more at
www.dk.com

Compass (19th century)

Drawing an ellipse

A demonstration to
show how different
elements behave in
the Solar System

Contents

French astronomical print (19th century)

The study of the heavens

THE WORD "ASTRONOMY" comes from a combination of two Greek words: *astron* meaning "star" and *nemein* meaning "to name." Even though the beginnings of astronomy go back thousands of years before the ancient Greeks began studying the stars, the science of astronomy has always been based on the same principle of "naming the stars." Many of the names come directly from the Greeks, since they were the first astronomers to make a systematic catalog of all the stars they could see. A number of early civilizations remembered the relative positions of the stars by putting together groups that seemed to make patterns in the night sky. One of these looked like a curling river, so it was called Eridanus, the great river; another looked like a hunter with a bright belt and dagger and was called Orion, the hunter (p. 61). Stars were named according to their placement inside the pattern and graded according to brightness. For example, the brightest star in the constellation Scorpius is called α *Scorpii*, because α is the first letter in the Greek alphabet. It is also called Antares, which means "the other Mars," because it shines bright red in the night sky and strongly resembles the blood-red planet, Mars (pp. 48-49).

WATCHING THE SKIES
The earliest astronomers were shepherds who watched the heavens for signs of the changing seasons. The clear nights would have given them opportunity to recognize familiar patterns and movements of the brightest heavenly bodies.

STUDYING THE STARS
Almost every culture made a study of the stars. During the so-called Dark Ages in Europe, the science of astronomy was kept alive by the Arabic-speaking peoples. The Greek star catalogs were improved and updated by the great Arabic astronomers, such as al-Sufi (903-986).

An engraving of al-Sufi with a celestial globe

UNCHANGING SKY
In all but the largest cities, where the stars are shrouded by pollution or hidden by the glare of streetlights, the recurring display of the night sky is still captivating. The view of the stars from the Earth has changed remarkably little during the past 10,000 years. The sky on any night in the 21st century is nearly the same as the one seen by people who lived thousands of years ago. The night sky for people of the early civilizations would have been more accessible because their lives were not as sheltered from the effects of nature as ours are. Despite the advances in the technology of astronomical observation, which include radio telescopes whose images appear on a computer screen, and telescopes launched into space to detect radiation that does not penetrate our atmosphere, there are still things the amateur astronomer can enjoy. Books and newspapers print star charts so that on a given night, in a specified geographic location, anyone looking upward into a clear sky can see the constellations for themselves.

TRADITIONAL SYMBOLS

The heritage of the Greek science of the stars passed through many different civilizations. In each case, the figures of the constellations took on the personalities of the heroes of local legends. The Mediterranean animals of the zodiac were transformed by other cultures, such as the Persians and Indians, into more familiar creatures, like the ibex, Brahma bulls, or a crayfish. This page is from an 18th-century Arabic manuscript. It depicts the zodiacal signs of Gemini, Cancer, Aries, and Taurus. The signs are in the Arabic script, which is read from right to left.

FROM SUPERSTITION TO SCIENCE

The science of astronomy grew out of a belief in astrology (pp. 16-17), the power of the planets and stars to affect life on the Earth. Each planet was believed to have the personality and powers of one of the gods. Mars, the god of war, shown here, determined war, plague, famine, and violent death.

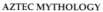

Quetzalcoatl

AZTEC MYTHOLOGY

In the Americas, the mythology of the stars was stronger than it was in Europe and Asia. This Aztec calendar shows the god Quetzalcoatl, who combined the influences of the Sun and Venus. His worship included ritual human sacrifice.

Light passes to the eye

LOOKING AT STARS

Many of the sky's mysteries can be seen with a good pair of binoculars. This 20th-century pair gave a better view of the heavens than either Newton, Galileo, or other great astronomers could have seen with their best telescopes (pp. 20-21).

Rays of light enter the objective lens

Two prisms fold up the light path

IMAGING SPACE

We can see 5,000 times farther into space than the ancients could. In 1990 NASA launched the first space telescope. The Hubble Space Telescope, orbiting beyond the Earth's atmosphere, can now produce high-resolution images of objects several billion light-years (p. 60) away. Among its tasks are pinpointing the areas near black holes and measuring the effect of gravity on starlight. Its faulty mirror was corrected and its solar panels replaced in 1993 in a spacewalk from the Space Shuttle (p. 35).

Ancient astronomy

BY WATCHING THE CYCLIC MOTION of the Sun, the Moon, and the stars, early observers soon realized that these repeating motions could be used to fashion the sky into a clock (to tell the passage of the hours of the day or night) and a calendar (to mark the progression of the seasons). Ancient monuments, such as Stonehenge in the UK and the pyramids of the Maya in Central America, offer evidence that the basic components of observational astronomy have been known for at least 6,000 years. With few exceptions, all civilizations have believed that the steady movements of the sky are the signal of some greater plan. The phenomenon of a solar eclipse (pp. 38-39), for example, was believed by some ancient civilizations to be a dragon eating the Sun. A great noise would successfully frighten the dragon away.

DEFYING THE HEAVENS
The ancient poets warn that you should never venture out to sea until the constellation of the Pleiades rises with the Sun in early May. If superpower leaders Mikhail Gorbachev and George Bush, Sr. had remembered their Greek poets, they would have known better than to try to meet on a boat in the Mediterranean in December 1989. Their summit was almost canceled because of bad weather.

PHASES OF THE MOON
The changing face of the Moon has always deeply affected people. The New Moon was considered the best time to start an enterprise, and the Full Moon was often feared as a time when spirits were free to roam. The word "lunatic" comes from the Latin name for the Moon, *luna*, because it was believed that the rays of the Full Moon caused insanity.

THE WORLD'S OLDEST OBSERVATORY
The earliest observatory to have survived is the Chomsung dae Observatory in Kyongju, Korea. A simple beehive structure, with a central opening in the roof, it resembles a number of prehistoric structures found all over the world. Many modern observatories (pp. 26-27) still have a similar roof opening.

NAMING THE PLANETS
The spread of knowledge tends to follow the two routes of trade and war. As great empires expanded, they brought their gods, customs, and learning with them. The earliest civilizations believed that the stars and planets were ruled by the gods. The Babylonians, for example, named each planet after the god that had most in common with that planet's characteristics. The Greeks and the Romans adopted the Babylonian system, replacing the names with those of their own gods. All the planet names can be traced directly to the Babylonian planet-gods: Nergal has become Mars, and Marduk has become the god Jupiter.

The Roman god Jupiter

Station stone

Aubrey holes are round pits that were part of the earliest structure

RECORDING THE SUN'S MOVEMENTS
Even though the precise significance of the standing stones at Stonehenge remains the subject of debate, it is clear from the arrangement of the stones that it was erected by prehistoric peoples specifically to record certain key celestial events, such as the summer and winter solstices and the spring and autumnal equinoxes. Although Stonehenge is the best known of the ancient megalithic monuments (those made of stone in prehistoric times), the sheer number of similar sites throughout the world underlines how many prehistoric peoples placed an enormous importance on recording the motions of the Sun and Moon.

BABYLONIAN RECORDS
The earliest astronomical records are in the form of clay tablets from ancient Mesopotamia and the great civilizations that flourished in the plains between the Tigris and Euphrates Rivers for more than 2,000 years. The oldest surviving astronomical calculations are relatively late, dating from the 4th century BC, but they are clearly based on generations of astronomical observations.

Back of a Persian astrolabe, 1707

Degree scale

Sight hole

Rotating alidade

Shadow square

Calendar scale

THE ASTROLABE
One of the problems faced by ancient astronomers was how to simplify the complex calculations needed to predict the positions of the planets and stars. One useful tool was the astrolabe, whose different engraved plates reproduce the sphere of the heavens in two dimensions. The alidade with its sight holes is used to measure the height of the Sun or the stars. By setting this against the calendar scale on the outside of the instrument, a number of different calculations can be made.

PLANNING THE HARVEST
For nearly all ancient cultures, the primary importance of astronomy was as a signal of seasonal changes. The Egyptians knew that when the star Sirius rose ahead of the Sun, the annual flooding of the Nile was not far behind. Schedules for planting and harvesting were all set by the Sun, the Moon, and the stars.

Arabic manuscript from the 14th century showing an astrolabe being used

Heel stone marks the original approach to Stonehenge

Avenue

Sun

Slaughter stone formed a ceremonial doorway

Altar stone

Station stone

Barrow

Circular bank and ditch

Circle of Sarsen stones with lintels

Ordering the Universe

A GREAT DEAL OF OUR KNOWLEDGE about the ancient science of astronomy comes from the Alexandrian Greek philosopher Claudius Ptolemaeus (c. AD 100-178), known as Ptolemy. He was an able scientist in his own right but, most importantly, he collected and clarified the work of all the great astronomers who had lived before him. He left two important sets of books. The *Almagest* was an astronomy textbook that provided an essential catalogue of all the known stars, updating Hipparchus. In the *Tetrabiblos*, Ptolemy discussed astrology. Both sets of books were the undisputed authority on their respective subjects for 1,600 years. Fortunately, they were translated into Arabic because, with the collapse of the Roman Empire around the 4th century, much accumulated knowledge disappeared as libraries were destroyed and books burned.

STAR CATALOGER
Hipparchus (190-120 BC) was one of the greatest of the Greek astronomers. He cataloged over 1,000 stars and developed the mathematical science of trigonometry. Here he is looking through a tube to help him concentrate on one area of the sky – the telescope was not yet invented (pp. 22-25).

Julius Caesar

THE LEAP YEAR
One of the problems confronting the astronomer-priests of antiquity was the fact that the lunar year and the solar year (p. 13) did not match up. By the middle of the 1st century BC, the Roman calendar was so mixed up that Julius Caesar (100-44 BC) ordered the Greek mathematician Sosigenes to develop a new system. He came up with the idea of a leap year every four years. This meant that the odd quarter day of the solar year was added in as one whole day once every four years.

Sirius, the dog star

FARNESE ATLAS
Very few images of the constellations have survived from antiquity. The main source for our knowledge is this 2nd-century Roman copy of an earlier Greek statue. The marble statue has the demi-god Atlas holding the heavens on his shoulders. All of the 48 Ptolemaic constellations are clearly marked in low relief.

Facsimile (1908) of the Behaim terrestrial globe

Europe
Red Sea
Ocean
Africa

SPHERICAL EARTH
The concept of a spherical Earth can be traced back to Greece in the 6th century BC. By Ptolemy's time, astronomers were accustomed to working with earthly (terrestrial) and starry (celestial) globes. The first terrestrial globe to be produced since antiquity, the 15th-century globe by Martin Behaim, shows an image of the Earth that is half based on myth. The Red Sea, for example, is colored red.

Navis, the Ship

Atlas

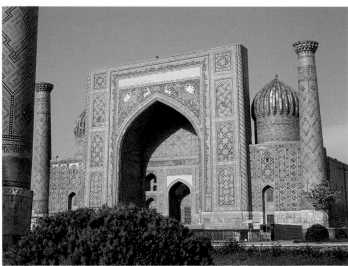

ARABIC SCHOOL OF ASTRONOMY
During the "Dark Ages," the great civilizations of Islam continued to develop the science of astronomy. Ulugh Beigh (c. 15th century) set up his observatory on this site in one of Asia's oldest cities – Samarkand, Uzbekistan. Here, measurements were made with the naked eye.

Geocentric Universe

It is logical to make assumptions from what your senses tell you. From the Earth it looks as if the heavens are circling over our heads. There is no reason to assume the Earth is moving at all. Ancient philosophers, naturally, believed that their Earth was stable and the center of the great cosmos. The planets were fixed to a series of crystalline spheres nested inside each other. The outermost sphere contained the stars.

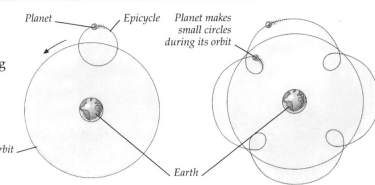

Planet   Epicycle   Planet makes small circles during its orbit

Orbit   Earth

THE EARTH AT THE CENTER

The geocentric or Earth-centered Universe is often referred to as the Ptolemaic Universe by later scholars to indicate that this was how classical scientists, like the great Ptolemy, believed the Universe was structured. He saw the Earth as the center of the Universe with the Moon, the known planets, and the Sun moving around it. Aristarchus (c. 310-230 BC) had already suggested that the Earth travels around the Sun, but his theory was rejected because it did not fit in with the mathematical and philosophical beliefs of the time.

Engraving (1490)
of the Ptolemaic Universe

PROBLEMS WITH THE GEOCENTRIC UNIVERSE

The main problem with the model of an Earth-centered Universe was that it did not help explain the apparently irrational behavior of some of the planets, which sometimes appear to stand still or move backward against the background of the stars (p. 19). Early civilizations assumed that these odd movements were signals from the gods, but the Greek philosophers spent centuries trying to develop rational explanations for what they saw. The most popular was the notion of epicycles. The planets moved in small circles (epicycles) on their orbits as they circled the Earth.

TEACHING TOOL

Astronomers have always found it difficult to explain the three-dimensional motions of the heavens. Ptolemy used something like this armillary sphere to do his complex astronomical calculations and to pass these ideas on to his students.

Equinoctial colure passes through the poles and the equinoxes

Arctic circle

Solstitial colure passes through the poles and the solstices

Ecliptic

Celestial equator

Moon

Earth

Meridian ring

Horizon ring

Sun

Tropic of Cancer

French painted armillary sphere (1770)

Stand

The celestial sphere

THE POSITIONS OF ALL OBJECTS IN SPACE are measured according to specific celestial coordinates. The best way to understand the cartography, or mapping, of the sky is to recall how the ancient philosophers imagined the Universe was shaped. They had no real evidence that the Earth moves, so they concluded that it was stationary and that the stars and planets revolve around it. They could see the stars wheeling around a single point in the sky and assumed that this must be one end of the axis of a great celestial sphere. They called it a crystalline sphere, or the sphere of fixed stars, because none of the stars seemed to change their positions relative to each other. The celestial coordinates used today come from this old-fashioned concept of a celestial sphere. The starry (celestial) and earthly (terrestrial) spheres share the same coordinates, such as a North and South Pole and an equator.

STAR TRAILS
A long photographic exposure of the sky taken from the northern hemisphere of the Earth shows the way in which stars appear to go in circles around the Pole Star or Polaris. Polaris is a bright star that lies within 1° of the true celestial pole, which, in turn, is located directly above the North Pole of the Earth. The rotation of the Earth on its north/south axis is the reason why the stars appear to move across the sky. Those closer to the Poles appear to move less than those further away.

Apex

Sight line   Peep hole

Peep hole

Pole Star

Great Bear

Horizontal plane

These two angles must add up to 90°

Degrees marked on arc

Angle read off where string crosses degree scale

Plumb bob

90°

MEASURING ALTITUDES
One of the earliest astronomical instruments is the quadrant. It is simply a quarter of a circle, whose curved edge has been divided into 90 degrees. Other similar instruments include the sextant which is one-sixth of a circle. By sighting the object through the peep holes along one straight edge of the quadrant, the observer can measure the height, or altitude, of that object. The altitude is the height in degrees (°) of a star above the horizon; it is not a linear measurement. A string with a plumb bob falls from the apex of the quadrant so that it intersects the divided arc. Since the angle between the vertical of the plumb bob and the horizontal plane of the horizon is 90°, simple mathematics can be used to work out the angle of sphe altitude.

DOING THE MATH
The apex of the quadrant is a 90° angle. As the sum of the angles of a triangle adds up to 180°, this means that the sum of the other two angles must add up to 90° too.

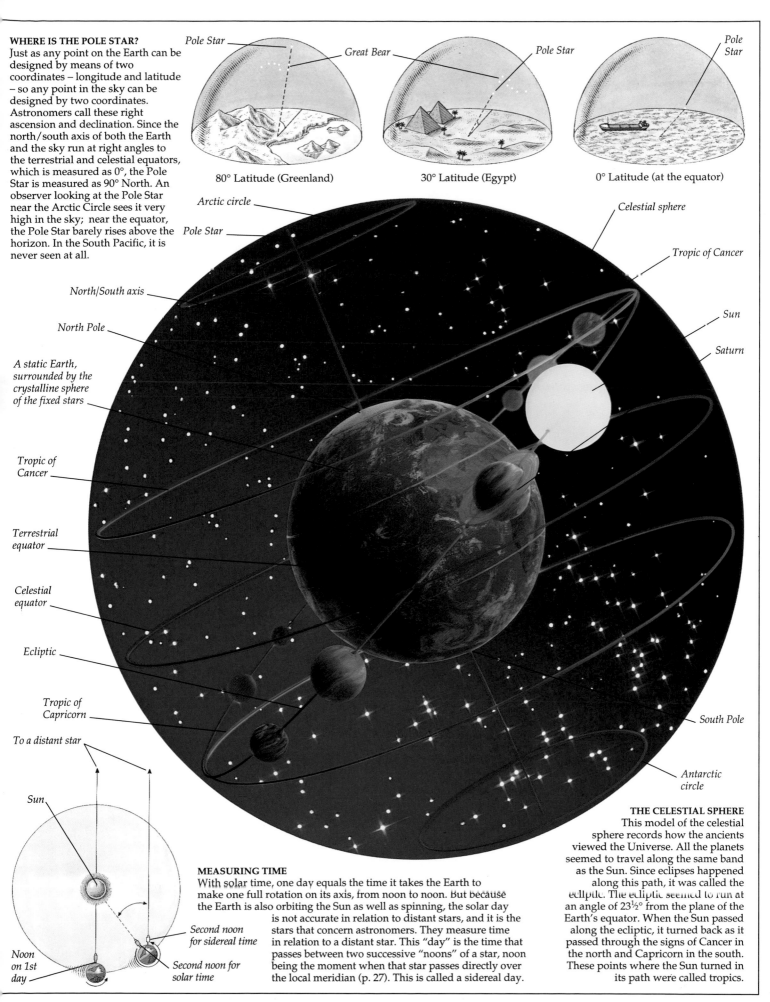

WHERE IS THE POLE STAR?
Just as any point on the Earth can be designed by means of two coordinates – longitude and latitude – so any point in the sky can be designed by two coordinates. Astronomers call these right ascension and declination. Since the north/south axis of both the Earth and the sky run at right angles to the terrestrial and celestial equators, which is measured as 0°, the Pole Star is measured as 90° North. An observer looking at the Pole Star near the Arctic Circle sees it very high in the sky; near the equator, the Pole Star barely rises above the horizon. In the South Pacific, it is never seen at all.

Pole Star

Great Bear

80° Latitude (Greenland)

Pole Star

30° Latitude (Egypt)

Pole Star

0° Latitude (at the equator)

Arctic circle

Pole Star

Celestial sphere

Tropic of Cancer

North/South axis

Sun

North Pole

Saturn

A static Earth, surrounded by the crystalline sphere of the fixed stars

Tropic of Cancer

Terrestrial equator

Celestial equator

Ecliptic

Tropic of Capricorn

South Pole

Antarctic circle

To a distant star

Sun

Second noon for sidereal time

Noon on 1st day

Second noon for solar time

MEASURING TIME
With solar time, one day equals the time it takes the Earth to make one full rotation on its axis, from noon to noon. But because the Earth is also orbiting the Sun as well as spinning, the solar day is not accurate in relation to distant stars, and it is the stars that concern astronomers. They measure time in relation to a distant star. This "day" is the time that passes between two successive "noons" of a star, noon being the moment when that star passes directly over the local meridian (p. 27). This is called a sidereal day.

THE CELESTIAL SPHERE
This model of the celestial sphere records how the ancients viewed the Universe. All the planets seemed to travel along the same band as the Sun. Since eclipses happened along this path, it was called the ecliptic. The ecliptic seemed to run at an angle of 23½° from the plane of the Earth's equator. When the Sun passed along the ecliptic, it turned back as it passed through the signs of Cancer in the north and Capricorn in the south. These points where the Sun turned in its path were called tropics.

13

The uses of astronomy

Sun

Alexandria

Syene

MEASURING THE EARTH
About 230 BC, Eratosthenes (c. 270-190 BC) estimated the size of the Earth by using the Sun. He discovered that the Sun was directly above his head at Syene in Upper Egypt at noon on the summer solstice. In Alexandria, directly north, the Sun was about 7° from its highest point (the zenith) at the summer solstice. Since Eratosthenes knew that the Earth is spherical (360° in circumference), the distance between the two towns should be 7/360ths of the Earth's circumference.

WITH ALL THE TOOLS OF MODERN TECHNOLOGY, it is sometimes hard to imagine how people performed simple functions such as telling time or knowing where they were on the Earth before the invention of clocks, maps, or navigational satellites. The only tools available were those provided by nature. The astronomical facts of the relatively regular interval of the day, the constancy of the movements of the fixed stars, and the assumption of certain theories, such as a spherical Earth, allowed people to measure their lives. By calculating the height of the Sun or certain stars, the ancient Greeks began to understand the shape and size of the Earth. In this way, they were able to determine their latitude. By plotting coordinates against a globe, they could fix their position on the Earth's surface. And by setting up carefully measured markers, or gnomons, they could begin to calculate the time of day.

Latitude scale

Sight hole

Sight hole

Movable cursor

Hour scale

AN ANCIENT SUNDIAL
Very early on, people realized that they could keep time by the Sun. Simple sundials like this allowed the traveler or merchant to know the local time for several different towns during a journey. The altitude of the Sun was measured through the sight holes in the bow and stern of the "little ship." When the cursor on the ship's mast was set to the correct latitude, the plumb bob would fall on the proper time.

Zodiac scale

Plumb bob

HOW A SUNDIAL WORKS
As the Sun travels across the sky, the shadow it casts changes in direction and length. A sundial works by setting a gnomon, or "indicator," so that the shadow the Sun casts at noon falls due north/south along a meridian. (A meridian is an imaginary line running from pole to pole; another name for meridian is a line of longitude.) The hours can then be divided before and after the noon mark. The terms AM and PM for morning and afternoon come from the Latin words meaning before and after the Sun passes the north/south meridian (*ante meridiem* and *post meridiem*).

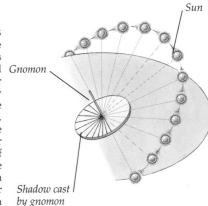

Sun

Gnomon

Shadow cast by gnomon at noon

Towns with their latitudes

Qiblah lid

FINDING MECCA
Part of Islamic worship is regular prayers, in which the faithful face toward the holy city of Mecca. The qiblah (direction of Mecca) indicator is a sophisticated instrument, developed during the Middle Ages to find the direction of Mecca. It also uses the Sun to determine the time for beginning and ending prayers.

TRAVELING TO THE SOUTH PACIFIC
It was thought that the early indigenous peoples of Polynesia were too "primitive" to have sailed the great distances between the north Pacific Ocean and New Zealand in the south. However, many tribes, including the Maoris of New Zealand, were capable of navigating thousands of miles using only the stars to guide them.

Rouen

Calais

Toulouse

Latitude marker

London

Latitude scale

Compass

CRUCIFORM SUNDIAL
Traveling Christian pilgrims often worried that any ornament might be considered a symbol of vanity. They solved this problem by incorporating religious symbolism into their sundials. This dial, shaped in the form of a cross, provided the means for telling the time in a number of English and French towns.

Magnetized needle

Degree scale

Compass bearing

Pointer

Argo, the ship

Hydra, the water snake

Argo Nauis

A CELESTIAL GLOBE

The celestial globe records the figures and stars of all the constellations against a grid of lines representing longitude and latitude. During the 17th and 18th centuries, all ships of the Dutch East India Company were given a matching pair of globes – terrestrial (p. 10) and celestial. Calculations could be made by comparing the coordinates on the two different globes. In practice, however, most navigators seemed to use flat sea charts to plot their journeys.

Meridian ring

Celestial globe 1618

The Southern Cross

Antarctic triangle

Centaurus, the Centaur

Sun

THE GREAT NAVIGATORS

Explorers of the 16th century had no idea what they would find when they set out to sea. Their heads were full of fables about mermaids and sea monsters. Even though this engraving of the Portuguese navigator Ferdinand Magellan (1480-1521) has many features that are clearly fantastical, it does show him using a pair of dividers to measure off an armillary sphere (p. 11). Beside the ship, the Sun God Apollo shines brightly; it was usually the Sun's position in the sky that helped a navigator find his latitude.

Shadow vane lined up with horizon vane

Horizon vane

Scale in degrees

Holder

Sight vane

Navigator with his back to the Sun

Horizon

Scale in degrees

USING A BACKSTAFF

The backstaff allowed a navigator to measure the height of the Sun without having to stare directly at it. The navigator held the instrument so that the shadow cast by the shadow vane would fall directly on to the horizon vane. Moving the sight vane, the navigator lined it up so he could see the horizon through the sight vane and the horizon vane. By adding together the angles of the sight and shadow vanes, the navigator could calculate the altitude of the Sun, from which he could determine the precise latitude of his ship.

Two angles give the Sun's altitude

90° angle

Horizon

DOING THE MATHEMATICS

To work out latitude at sea, a navigator needs to find the altitude of the Sun at noon. He doesn't even need to know the time; as long as the Sun is at its highest point in the sky, the altitude can be measured with a backstaff or other instrument (p. 12). Then, using nautical tables of celestial coordinates, he can find his latitude with a simple equation using the angle of altitude and the coordinates of the Sun in the celestial sphere (p. 13).

Astrology

THE WORD "ASTROLOGY" comes from the Greek *astron* meaning "star" and *logos* meaning "the science." Since Babylonian times, people staring at the night sky were convinced that the regular motions of the heavens were indications of some great cosmic purpose. Priests and philosophers believed that if they could map the stars and their movements, they could decode these messages and understand the patterns that had an effect on past and future events. What was originally observational astronomy – observing the stars and planets – gradually grew into the astrology that has today become a regular part of many people's lives. However, there is no evidence that the stars and planets have any effect on our personalities or our destinies. Astronomers now think astrology is superstition. Its original noble motives should not be forgotten, however. For most of the so-called Dark Ages, when all pure science was in deep hibernation, it was astrology and the desire to know about the future that kept the science of astronomy alive.

THE ASTROLOGER
In antiquity, the astrologer's main task was to predict the future. This woodcut, dating from 1490, shows two astrologers working with arrangements of the Sun, Moon, and planets to find the astrological effects on peoples' lives.

RULERSHIP OVER ORGANS
Until the discoveries of modern medicine, people believed that the body was governed by four different types of essences called "humors." An imbalance in these humors would lead to illness. Each of the 12 signs of the zodiac (right) had special links with each of the humors and with parts of the human body. So, for example, for a headache due to moisture in the head (a cold), treatment would be with a drying agent – some plant ruled by the Sun or an "Earth sign," like Virgo – when a New Moon was well placed toward the sign of Aries, which ruled the head.

Dates in the month

Days in the week

Father Time

Back of calendar

Hours of daylight

Time of sunrise

Hours of night time

Time of sunset

PERPETUAL CALENDAR
The names for the days of the week show traces of astrological belief – for example, Sunday is the Sun's day, and Monday is the Moon's day. This simple perpetual calendar, which has small planetary signs next to each day, shows the day of the week for any given date. The user can find the day by turning the inner dial to a given month or date and reading off the information.

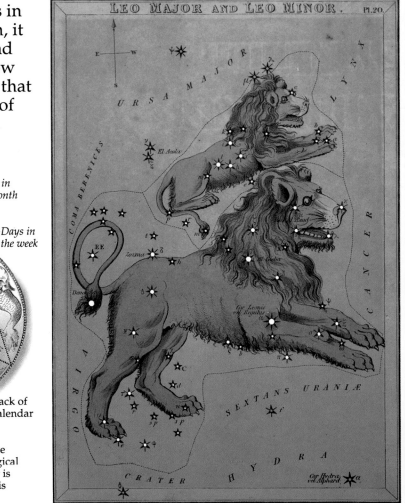

LEO, THE LION
These 19th-century French constellation cards show each individual star marked with a hole through which light shines. Astrologically, each zodiacal sign has its own properties and its own friendships and enemies within the zodiacal circle. Each sign is also ruled by a planet, which similarly has its own properties, friendships, and enemies. So, for example, a person born while the Sun is passing through Leo is supposed to be kingly, like a lion.

PLANETARY POSITIONS

One way in which planets are supposed to be in or out of harmony with one another depends on their relative positions in the heavens. When two planets are found within a few degrees of each other, they are said to be in conjunction. When planets are separated by exactly 180° in the zodiacal band, they are said to be in opposition.

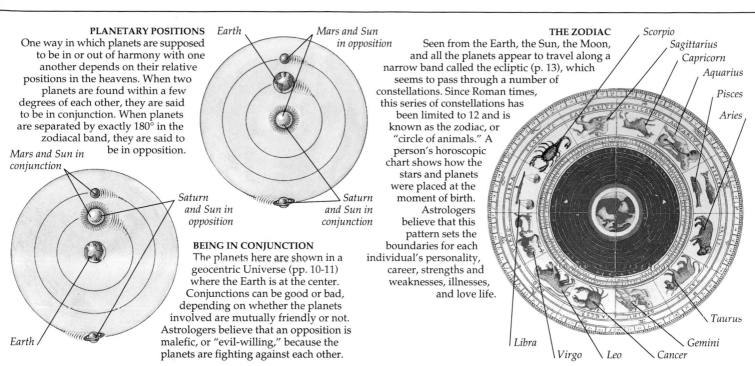

Earth

Mars and Sun in opposition

Mars and Sun in conjunction

Saturn and Sun in opposition

Saturn and Sun in conjunction

Earth

BEING IN CONJUNCTION

The planets here are shown in a geocentric Universe (pp. 10-11) where the Earth is at the center. Conjunctions can be good or bad, depending on whether the planets involved are mutually friendly or not. Astrologers believe that an opposition is malefic, or "evil-willing," because the planets are fighting against each other.

THE ZODIAC

Seen from the Earth, the Sun, the Moon, and all the planets appear to travel along a narrow band called the ecliptic (p. 13), which seems to pass through a number of constellations. Since Roman times, this series of constellations has been limited to 12 and is known as the zodiac, or "circle of animals." A person's horoscopic chart shows how the stars and planets were placed at the moment of birth. Astrologers believe that this pattern sets the boundaries for each individual's personality, career, strengths and weaknesses, illnesses, and love life.

Scorpio
Sagittarius
Capricorn
Aquarius
Pisces
Aries
Taurus
Gemini
Cancer
Leo
Virgo
Libra

SCORPIO, THE SCORPION

Most of the constellations are now known by the Latinized versions of their original Greek names. This card shows Scorpius, or Scorpio. This is the sign "through which" the Sun passes between late October and late November. Astrologers believe that people born during this time of year are intuitive, yet secretive, like a scorpion scuttling under a rock.

CANCER, THE CRAB

Someone who is born while the Sun is transitting the constellation Cancer is supposed to be a homebody, like a crab in its shell. These hand-painted cards are collectively known as *Urania's Mirror* – Urania is the name of the muse of astronomy (p. 19). By holding the cards up to the light, it is possible to learn the shapes and relative brightness of the stars in each constellation.

The Copernican revolution

I<small>N</small> 1543 N<small>ICOLAUS</small> C<small>OPERNICUS</small> published a book that changed the perception of the Universe. In his *De revolutionibus orbium coelestium* ("Concerning the revolutions of the celestial orbs"), Copernicus argued that the Sun, and not the Earth, is at the center of the Universe. It was a heliocentric Universe, *helios* being the Greek word for Sun. His reasoning was based on the logic of the time. He argued that a sphere moves in a circle that has no beginning and no end. Since the Universe and all the heavenly bodies are spherical, their motions must be circular and uniform. In the Ptolemaic, Earth-centered system (pp. 10-11), the paths of the planets are irregular. Copernicus assumed that uniform motions in the orbits of the planets appear irregular to us because the Earth is not at the center of the Universe. These discoveries were put forward by many different astronomers, but they ran against the teachings of both the Protestant and Catholic churches. In 1616 all books written by Copernicus and any others that put the Sun at the center of the Universe were condemned by the Catholic Church.

NICOLAUS COPERNICUS
The Polish astronomer Nicolaus Copernicus (1473-1543) made few observations. Instead, he read the ancient philosophers and discovered that none of them had been able to agree about the structure of the Universe.

Sun

Zodiac

COPERNICAN UNIVERSE
Copernicus based the order of his Solar System on how long it took each planet to complete a full orbit. This early print shows the Earth in orbit around the Sun with the Zodiac beyond.

THE GREAT OBSERVER
The Danish astronomer Tycho Brahe (1546-1601) discovered a new star – a nova – in the constellation of Cassiopeia in 1572. The star was so bright that it was visible even during the day. This appearance challenged the inherited wisdom from the ancients, which claimed that the stars were eternal and unchanging. To study what this appearance might mean, a new observatory was set up near Copenhagen in Denmark. Brahe re-measured 788 stars of Ptolemy's great star catalog, thereby producing the first complete, modern stellar atlas.

Uranibourg, Tycho's observatory on the island of Hven

DRAWING AN ELLIPSE
An ellipse can be drawn by pushing two pins into a board and linking them with a loop of thread. When a pencil is placed within the loop and moved around the pins, keeping the loop tight, the shape it makes is an ellipse. The position of each pin is called a focus. In the Solar System the Sun is at one focus of the ellipse in a planetary orbit. The wider apart the pins are placed, the more eccentric the planetary orbit (pp. 36-37).

Thread loop

Pin

Pin

Focus

Focus

Ellipse

LAWS OF PLANETARY MOTION
Johannes Kepler (above right) added the results of his own observations to Tycho's improved planetary and stellar measurements. Kepler discovered that the orbits of the planets were not perfectly circular, as had been believed for 1,600 years. They were elliptical, with the Sun placed at one focus of the ellipse (left). While observing the orbit of Mars, Kepler discovered that there are variations in its speed. At certain points in its orbit, Mars seemed to be traveling faster than at other times. He soon realized that the Sun was regulating the orbiting speed of the planet. When it is closest to the Sun – its perihelion – the planet orbits most quickly; at its aphelion – farthest from the Sun – it slows down.

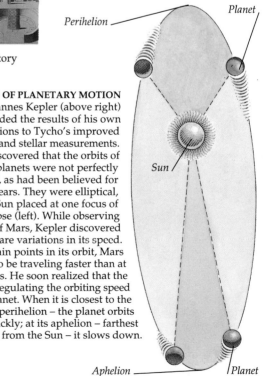

Perihelion

Planet

Sun

Aphelion

Planet

JOHANNES KEPLER (1571-1630)
It was due to the intervention of Tycho Brahe that the German mathematician Johannes Kepler landed the prestigious position of Imperial Mathematician in 1601. Tycho left all his papers to Kepler, who was a vigorous supporter of the Copernican heliocentric system. Kepler formulated three laws of planetary motion and urged Galileo (pp. 20) to publish his research in order to help prove the Copernican thesis.

Planet paths shown in a planetarium

APPARENT PATHS
The irregular motion that disproved the geocentric universe was the retrograde motion of the planets. From an earthly perspective, some of the planets – particularly Mars – seem to double back on their orbits, making great loops in the night sky. (The light display above draws the apparent orbit of Mars.) Ptolemy proposed that retrograde motion could be explained by planets travelling on smaller orbits (p. 11). Once astronomers realized that the Sun is the center of the Solar System, the apparent path of Mars, for example, could be explained. But first it had to be understood that the Earth has a greater orbiting speed than that of Mars, which appeared to slip behind. Even though the orbit of Mars seems to keep pace with the Earth (below left), the apparent path is very different (above left).

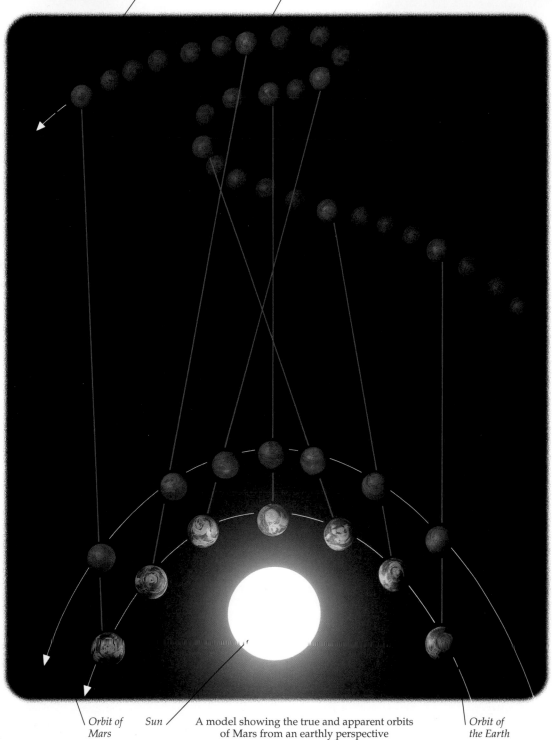

Apparent path of Mars   *Line of sight*

Orbit of Mars   *Sun*   A model showing the true and apparent orbits of Mars from an earthly perspective   *Orbit of the Earth*

WEIGHING UP THE THEORIES
This engraving from a 17th-century manuscript shows Urania, the muse of astronomy, comparing the different theoretical systems for the arrangement of the Universe. Ptolemy's system is at her feet, and Kepler's is outweighed by Tycho's system on the right.

Intellectual giants

It takes both luck and courage to be a radical thinker. Galileo Galilei (1564-1642) had the misfortune of being brilliant at a time when new ideas were considered dangerous. His numerous discoveries, made with the help of the newly invented telescope, provided ample support for the Copernican heliocentric, or Sun-centered, Universe (pp. 18-19). Galileo's findings about the satellites of Jupiter (p. 50) and the phases of Venus clearly showed that the Earth could not be the center of all movement in the Universe and that the heavenly bodies were not perfect in their behavior. For this Galileo was branded a heretic and sentenced to a form of life imprisonment. The great English physicist Isaac Newton (1642-1727), born the year Galileo died, had both luck and courage. He lived in an age enthusiastic for new ideas, especially those related to scientific discovery.

GALILEO'S TELESCOPE
Galileo never claimed to have invented the telescope. In *Il saggiatore*, "The Archer," he commends the "simple spectacle-maker" who "found the instrument" by chance. When he heard of Lippershey's results (p. 22), Galileo reinvented the instrument from the description of its effects. His first telescope magnified at eight times. Within a few days, however, he had constructed a telescope with x 20 magnification. He went on to increase his magnification to x 30, having ground the lenses himself.

POPE URBAN VIII
Originally, the Catholic Church had welcomed Copernicus's work (pp. 18-19). However, by 1563 the Church was becoming increasingly strict and abandoned its previously lax attitude toward any deviation from established doctrine. Pope Urban VIII was one of the many caught in this swing. As a cardinal, he had been friendly with Galileo and often had Galileo's book, *Il saggiatore*, read to him aloud at meals. In 1635, however, he authorized the Grand Inquisition of Galileo's research.

LOOKING AT THE MOON'S SURFACE
Through his telescope, Galileo measured the shadows on the Moon to show how the mountains there were much taller than those on Earth. These ink sketches were published in his book *Sidereus nuncius*, "Messenger of the Stars," in 1610.

RENAISSANCE MAN
In 1611 Galileo traveled to Rome to discuss his findings about the Sun and its position in the Universe with the leaders of the Church. They accepted his discoveries, but not the theory that underpinned them – the Copernican, heliocentric Universe (pp. 18-19). Galileo was accused of heresy and, in 1635, condemned for disobedience and sentenced to house arrest until his death in 1642. He was pardoned in 1992.

PHASES OF VENUS
From his childhood days, Galileo was characterized as the sort of person who was unwilling to accept facts without evidence. In 1610, by applying the telescope to astronomy, he discovered the moons of Jupiter and the phases of Venus. He immediately understood that the phases of Venus are caused by the Sun shining on a planet that revolves around it. He knew that this was proof that the Earth was not the center of the Universe. He hid his findings in a Latin anagram, or word puzzle, as he did with many of the discoveries that he knew would be considered "dangerous" by the authorities.

PATH OF A PROJECTILE
Medieval philosophers did not understand the motion of projectiles, such as a cannonball fired from a cannon. It was Galileo who first studied the path of projectiles. In reality, a projectile (the cannonball) is continually pulled downward due to gravity. At the point of firing, the cannonball travels upward, slows down, and stops before being pulled downward by gravity. If something is fired with enough force (like a rocket), it will circle the Earth.

The ball travels upward

The ball slows down

The ball is pulled down

The fastest ball moves the farthest

NEWTON AND LIGHT
In 1666, when Newton was only 25 years old, he bought a triangular prism in order to study the "phenomenon of colors," as he first described the effect of white light breaking into a spectrum. He noticed that even though the white light had come through a tiny hole in his shutters, the spectrum it created was elongated, with the blue end of the spectrum more severely bent than the red one. His findings were to have far-reaching effects in the development of the telescope (pp. 22-25) and the science of spectroscopy (pp. 30-31).

Incoming light

Eyepiece

Side view of a replica of
Newton's reflecting telescope

THE MOON AND GRAVITY
When Newton saw an apple fall from a tree he realized that the power of gravity, which had brought the apple from the tree to the ground, might extend much farther – even to the Moon. Like the apple, the Moon is held in its orbit because it is constantly "falling" toward the Earth. Gravity holds it in check; otherwise, it would hurtle in a straight line out into space.

Earth

Moon's orbit

Moon

Force of gravity

Moon would hurtle into space without gravity

NEWTON'S REFLECTOR
The design of Newton's telescope was a direct result of his experiments with light. He knew that a lens could break down white light into its constituent parts and cause chromatic aberration, or haloes of colored light (p. 23), around the object viewed. By using mirrors instead of lenses in his reflecting telescopes, he avoided this problem altogether. His invention, published by England's Royal Society in 1671, made him instantly famous throughout Europe.

Barycenter

Two bodies of similar density

Earth

Barycenter

Moon

The Earth and the Moon

THE BARYCENTER
Newton realized that the force that made things fall and kept planets in orbit around the Sun was the same – a gravitational attraction. Two bodies in orbit move about a point that is the center of their two masses – the "barycenter" or balancing point between the two. Two spheres of equal mass have a barycenter midway between them. If the Earth and the Moon had the same density (p. 45), their barycenter would be outside the larger body. Because the Earth has a greater density than that of the Moon, the balancing point is just inside the Earth.

Sliding focus

Wooden ball mounting

Objective mirror

Secondary mirror

Objective mirror

Front view
of reflecting
telescope

Optical principles

Pᴇᴏᴘʟᴇ ʜᴀᴠᴇ ʙᴇᴇɴ ᴀᴡᴀʀᴇ of the magnifying properties of a curved piece of glass since at least 2,000 ʙᴄ. The Greek philosopher Aristophanes in the 5th century ʙᴄ had used a glass globe filled with water in order to magnify the fine print in his manuscripts. In the middle of the 13th century the English scientist Roger Bacon (1214-1292) proposed that the "lesser segment of a sphere of glass or crystal" will make small objects appear clearer and larger. For this suggestion, Bacon's colleagues branded him a dangerous magician and imprisoned for 10 years. Even though eyeglasses were invented in Italy some time between 1285 and 1300, superstitions were not overcome for another 250 years when scientists discovered the combination of lenses that would lead to the invention of the telescope. There were two types of telescope. The refracting telescope uses lenses to bend light; the reflecting telescope uses mirrors to reflect the light back to the observer.

Viewer | Concave eyepiece lens

INVENTOR OF THE TELESCOPE
It is believed that the first real telescope was invented in 1608 in Holland by the glasses maker Hans Lippershey from Zeeland. According to the story, two of Lippershey's children were playing in his shop and noticed that by holding two lenses in a straight line they could magnify the weather vane on the local church. Lippershey placed the two lenses in a tube and claimed the invention of the telescope. In the mid 1550s an Englishman Leonard Digges had created a primitive instrument that, with a combination of mirrors and lenses, could reflect and enlarge objects viewed through it. There was controversy about whether this was a true scientific telescope or not. It was Galileo (p. 20) who adapted the telescope to astronomy.

Decorative ribbons might be attached here

Horn lens holder

Convex lens

EARLY EYEGLASSES (1750)
Most early glasses like these had convex lenses. These helped people who were farsighted to focus on objects close at hand. Later, glasses were made with concave lenses for those who were nearsighted.

Water

Path of light is bent again on reentering air

Light is bent

Light from laser

HOW REFRACTION WORKS
Light usually travels in a straight line, but it can be bent or "refracted" by passing it through substances of differing densities. This laser beam (here viewed from overhead) seems to bend as it is directed at a rectangular-shaped container of water because the light is passing through three different media – water, glass, and air.

Reflected light beam | *Light from laser is bent back by a shiny surface* | *Incident light beam*

HOW REFLECTION WORKS
The word reflection comes from the Latin *reflectere*, meaning to "bend back." A shiny surface will bend back rays of light that strike it. The rays approaching the mirror are called incident rays and those leaving it are called outgoing, or reflected, rays. The angle at which the incident rays hit the mirror is the same as the angle of the reflected rays leaving it. What the eye sees are the light rays reflected in the mirror.

Large concave mirror

CHROMATIC ABERRATION
When light goes through an ordinary lens, each color in the spectrum is bent at a different angle causing rainbows to appear around the images viewed. The blue end of the spectrum will bend more sharply than the red end of the spectrum so that the two colors will focus at different points. This is chromatic aberration. By adding a second lens made from a different kind of glass (and with a different density), all the colors focus at the same point and the problem is corrected.

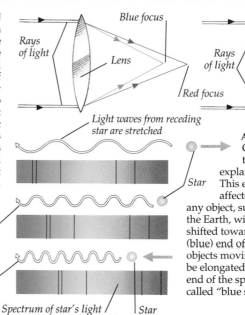

Rays of light *Blue focus* *Lens* *Red focus*

Both colors at same focus *Rays of light* *Two lenses*

JOHN DOLLOND
The English optician John Dollond (1706-1761) was the first to perfect the achromatic lens so that it might be manufactured more easily and solve the problem of chromatic aberration. Dollond claimed to have invented a new method of refraction.

Light waves from receding star are stretched

Earth

Light waves from a stationary star

Light waves from star approaching the Earth are compressed

Star

Spectrum of star's light *Star*

AN EFFECT OF LIGHT
One effect of light viewed through a telescope can be explained by the Doppler effect. This explains how wavelength is affected by motion. The light of any object, such as a star approaching the Earth, will be compressed and shifted toward the short wavelength (blue) end of the spectrum. Light from objects moving away from the Earth will be elongated and shifted toward the red end of the spectrum. These effects are called "blue shift" and "red shift."

A REFRACTING TELESCOPE
In a refracting telescope, the convex objective lens (the one farthest from the eye) collects the light and forms an image. The convex eyepiece lens (the one closest to the eye) magnifies the image in just the same way as a magnifying glass. Galileo used a similar type of refracting telescope (p. 20). The main problem with the refracting telescope is chromatic aberration (above).

A REFLECTING TELESCOPE
Sir Isaac Newton (p. 21) developed a version of the reflecting telescope that consists of a large concave, or curved, mirror to catch the light. The mirror then sends the light back to an inclined flat, or plane, mirror where the image is formed. The eyepiece lens magnifies the image. Unlike the lenses in a refracting telescope, the mirrors in a reflecting telescope do not cause chromatic aberration, so the image is clearer.

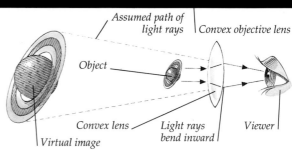

Viewer *Eyepiece lens*

Assumed path of light rays *Convex objective lens* *Object* *Convex lens* *Light rays bend inward* *Viewer* *Virtual image*

HOW A LENS MAGNIFIES
When a convex lens is held between the eye and an object, the object appears larger because the lens bends the rays of light inward. The eye naturally traces the rays of light back toward the object in straight lines. It sees a "virtual" image, which is larger than the original image. The degree of magnification depends on the angles formed by the curvature of the lens.

Plane mirror *Incoming light*

The optical telescope

THE MORE LIGHT THAT REACHES THE EYEPIECE in a telescope, the brighter the image of the heavens will be. Astronomers made their lenses and mirrors bigger, changed the focal length of the telescopes, and combined honeycombs of smaller mirrors to make a single, large reflective surface in order to capture the greatest amount of light and focus it onto a single point. During the 19th century, refracting telescopes (pp. 22-23) were preferred, and opticians devoted themselves to perfecting large lenses free of blemishes.
In the 20th century there were advances in materials and mirror coatings. Large mirrors collect more light than small ones, but are also heavier. They may even sag under their own weight, distorting the image. One solution is segmented-mirror telescopes, in which many smaller mirrors are mounted side by side. Another is "active optics," where mirrors move to compensate for any sagging.

CAMERAS ON TELESCOPES
Since the 19th century, astronomical photography has been an important tool for astronomers. By attaching a camera to a telescope that has been specially adapted with a motor that can be set to keep the telescope turning at the same speed as the rotation of the Earth, the astronomer can take very long exposures of distant stars (p. 12). Before the invention of photography, astronomers had to draw everything they saw. They had to be artists as well as scientists.

Eyepiece

Eyepiece mounting

Handle for adjusting angle of tube

HERSCHEL'S TELESCOPE
First out of economic necessity and later as an indication of his perfectionism, English astronomer William Herschel (1738-1822) always built his telescopes and hand-ground his own lenses and mirrors. The magnification of a telescope like his 6-in (15-cm) Newtonian reflector is about 200 times. This wooden telescope is the kind he would have used during his great survey of the sky, during which he discovered the planet Uranus (pp. 54-55).

Guide rails for raising telescope

Telescope tube

Objective mirror located inside the tube

Drawer for notes

Handles for raising and lowering telescope

The mounting

Wheeled base

MORE MAGNIFICATION
Increasing the magnification of telescopes was one of the major challenges facing early astronomers. Since the technology to make large lenses was not sufficiently developed, the only answer was to make telescopes with a very long distance between the eyepiece lens and the objective lens. In some instances, this led to telescopes of ridiculous proportions, as shown in this 18th-century engraving. These long focal-length telescopes were impossible to use. The slightest vibration caused by someone walking past would make the telescope tremble so violently that observations were impossible.

Holders for thread

Calibrations

Screw

MEASURING ACROSS VAST DISTANCES

The bigger the telescope, the larger its scale will be. This means that measurements become increasingly crude. A micrometer can be set to provide extremely fine gradations, a necessary element when measuring the distances between two stars in the sky that are a very long way away. This micrometer was made by William Herschel. To pinpoint the location of a star, a fine hair or spiderweb was threaded between two holders that were adjusted by means of the finely turned screw on the side.

AN EQUATORIAL MOUNT

Telescopes have to be mounted in some way. The equatorial mount used to be the favored mount, and is still preferred by amateur astronomers. The telescope is lined up with the Earth's axis, using the Pole Star as a guide. In the southern hemisphere, other stars near the sky's south pole are used. The telescope can swing around this axis, automatically following the tracks of stars in the sky as they circle around the Pole Star. The equatorial mount was used for this 28-in (71-cm) refractor, installed at Greenwich in 1893.

Pivot point

Graduated scales of arc

Ladder for an astronomer to reach the eyepiece

ASTRONOMICAL QUADRANT

Most early telescopes were mounted on astronomical quadrants (p. 12), and to stabilize the telescope, the quadrant was usually mounted on a wall. These kinds of telescopes are called mural quadrants from the Latin word for "wall," *murus*. The telescope was hung on a single pivot-point, so that its eyepiece could be moved along the graduated scale of the arc of the quadrant (p. 12). In this way, astronomers could accurately measure the altitude of the stars they were observing.

GEMINI TELESCOPE

There are two Gemini Telescopes, one in Hawaii (in the northern hemisphere) and one in Chile (in the southern hemisphere). Together they give optical and infrared coverage of the whole sky. Each Gemini Telescope has a single active mirror that is 26.6 ft (8.1 m) across. The mirrors have protected silver coatings that help to prevent interference in the infrared spectrum.

GRINDING MIRRORS

The 16-ft (5-m) mirror of the famous Hale telescope on Mount Palomar in California was cast in 1934 from 35 tons of molten Pyrex. The grinding of the mirror to achieve the correct curved shape was interrupted by World War II. It was not completed until 1947. Mount Palomar was one of the first high-altitude observatories, built where the atmosphere is thinner and the effects of pollution are reduced.

A SEGMENTED-MIRROR TELESCOPE

Inside each of the twin Keck Telescopes in Hawaii, there is a primary six-sided mirror that is around 33 ft (10 m) wide. It is made up of 36 smaller hexagonal mirrors, which are 6 ft (1.8 m) across. Each small mirror is monitored by a computer, and its position can be adjusted to correct any sagging. The two telescopes are also linked so that they can combine their signals for an even more accurate image.

Observatories

Aを OBSERVATORY IS A PLACE where astronomers watch the heavens. The shapes of observatories have changed greatly over the ages (p. 8). The earliest were quiet places set atop city walls or in towers. Height was important so that the astronomer could have a panoramic, 360° view of the horizon. The Babylonians and the Greeks certainly had rudimentary observatories, but the greatest of the early observatories were those in Islamic North Africa and the Middle East – Baghdad, Cairo, and Damascus. The great observatory in Baghdad had a huge 20-ft (6-m) quadrant and a 56-ft (17-m) stone sextant. It must have looked very much like the observatory in Jaipur – the only one of this type of observatory to remain relatively intact (below). As the great Islamic empires waned and science reawakened in western Europe, observatories took on a different shape. The oldest observatory still in use is the Observatoire de Paris, founded in 1667 (p. 28). A less hospitable climate meant that open-air observatories were impractical. The astronomer and the instruments needed a roof over their heads. Initially, these roofs were constructed with sliding panels or doors that could be pulled back to open the building to the night sky. Since the 19th century, most large telescopes are covered with huge rotatable domes. The earliest domes were made of papier mâché, the onl substance known to be sufficiently light and strong. Now most domes are made of aluminum.

THE LEVIATHAN OF PARSONSTOWN
William Parsons (1800-1867), the third Earl of Rosse, was determined to build the largest reflecting telescope. At Parsonstown in Ireland he managed to cast a 72-in (182-cm) mirror, weighing nearly 4 tons and magnifying 800-1,000 times. When the "Leviathan" was built in 1845, it was used by Parsons to make significant discoveries concerning the structure of galaxies and nebulae (pp. 60-63).

BEIJING OBSERVATORY
The Great Observatory set on the walls of the Forbidden City in Beijing, China, was constructed with the help of Jesuit priests from Portugal in 1660 on the site of an older observatory. The instruments included two great armillary spheres (p. 11), a huge celestial globe (p. 10), a graduated azimuth horizon ring, and an astronomical quadrant and sextant (p. 12). The shapes of these instruments were copied from woodcut illustrations in Tycho Brahe's *Mechanica* of 1598 (p. 18).

JAIPUR, INDIA
Early observations were carried out by the naked eye from the top of monumental architectural structures. The observatory at Jaipur in Rajahstan, India, was built by Maharajah Jai Singh in 1726. The monuments include a massive sundial, the Samrat Yantra, and a gnomon inclined at 27°, showing the latitude of Jaipur and the height of the Pole Star (p. 13). There is also a large astronomical sextant and a meridian chamber.

MAUNA KEA
Increasing use of artificial light and air pollution from the world's populous cities have driven astronomers to the most uninhabited regions of the Earth to build their observatories. The best places are mountain tops or deserts in temperate climates, where the air is dry, stable, and without clouds. The Mauna Kea volcano on the island of Hawaii has the thinner air of high altitudes and the temperate climate of the Pacific. There are optical, infrared, and radio telescopes there.

COMPUTER-DRIVEN TELESCOPE
Telescopes have become so big that astronomers are dwarfed by them. This 20-in (51-cm) solar coronagraph in the Crimean Astrophysical Observatory in the Ukraine is driven by computer-monitored engines. A coronagraph is a type of solar telescope that measures the outermost layers of the Sun's atmosphere (p. 38).

What is a meridian?

Meridian lines are imaginary coordinates running from pole to pole that are used to measure distances east and west on the Earth's surface and in the heavens. Meridian lines are also known as lines of longitude. The word meridian comes from the Latin word *meridies*, meaning "the mid-day," because the Sun crosses a local meridian at noon. Certain meridians became important because astronomers used them in observatories when they set up their telescopes for positional astronomy. This means that all their measurements of the sky and the Earth were made relative to their local meridian. Until the end of the 19th century, there were a number of national meridians in observatories in Paris, Cadiz, and Naples.

Prime meridian

THE GREENWICH MERIDIAN
In 1884 there was an international conference in Washington to choose a single Zero Meridian, or Prime Meridian, for the world. The meridian running through the Airy Transit Circle – a telescope mounted so that it rotated in a north/south plane – at the Royal Greenwich Observatory outside London was chosen. This choice was largely a matter of convenience. Most of the shipping charts and all of the American railroad system used Greenwich as their longitude zero at the time. South of Greenwich, the Prime Meridian crosses through France and Africa, and then runs across the Atlantic Ocean all the way to the South Pole.

CROSSING THE MERIDIAN
In 1850 the 7th Astronomer Royal of Great Britain, Sir George Biddle Airy (1801-1892), decided he wanted a new telescope. In building it, he moved the previous Prime Meridian for England 19 ft (5.75 m) to the east. The Greenwich Meridian is marked by an illuminated line which bisects Airy's Transit Circle at the Old Royal Observatory (now a museum).

The astronomer

THE MAIN DIFFERENCE BETWEEN ASTRONOMERS and other scientists is that astronomers are not in a position to make things happen. The astronomer has to wait and watch – the key to all astronomy is observing, whether through an optical telescope or by scanning a digitized readout from a computer. There are many different kinds of astronomers. Positional astronomers are mostly interested in measuring the relative positions of the stars. They make the two-dimensional maps of the heavens. Astrophysicists are astronomers who try to understand the physics of the Universe and how matter behaves in the extremes of space. But the types of questions asked by astrophysicists can be traced directly back to the questions of the earliest Greek philosophers – what is the Universe, how is it shaped, and how do I fit into it?

FASHIONABLE AMATEURS
By the 18th century, the science of the stars became an acceptable pastime for the rich and sophisticated. The large number of small telescopes that survive from this period are evidence of how popular amateur astronomy became.

THE NAUTICAL ALMANAC
First published in 1766, *The Nautical Almanac* provides a series of tables showing the distances between certain key stars and the Moon at three-hourly intervals. Navigators can use the tables to help calculate their longitude at sea, when they are out of sight of land (p. 27).

FIRST ASTRONOMER ROYAL
England appointed its first Astronomer Royal, John Flamsteed (1646-1719), in 1675. He lived and worked at the Royal Observatory, Greenwich, built by King Charles II of England in the same year.

IN THE FAMILY
When the Observatoire de Paris was founded in 1667, the French King called a well-known Bolognese astronomer, Gian Domenico Cassini (1625-1712), to be the observatory's director. He was followed by three generations of Cassinis in the position: Jacques Cassini (1677-1756); César-François Cassini de Thury (1714-1784), who produced the first modern map of France; and Jean-Dominique Cassini (1748-1845). Most historians refer to this great succession of astronomers simply as Cassini I, Cassini II, Cassini III, and Cassini IV.

ASTRONOMY IN RUSSIA
The Russian astronomer Mikhail Lomonosov (1711-1765) was primarily interested in problems relating to the art of navigation and in fixing latitude and longitude. During his observations of the 1761 Transit of Venus (pp. 46-47), he noticed that the planet seemed "smudgy" and suggested that Venus had a thick atmosphere, many times denser than that of the Earth.

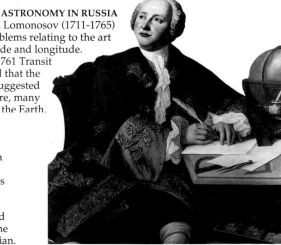

Peg marking α Cassiopiae   *Peg marking α Aquarii*   *Rotating clock face*

Peg marking Antares

Peg marking α Hydrae

STAR CLOCK (1815)
One of the primary aspects of positional astronomy is measuring a star's position against a clock. This ingenious clock has the major stars inscribed on the surface of its rotating face. Placing pegs in the holes near the stars to be observed causes the clock to chime when the star is due to pass the local meridian.

NAPIER'S BONES

One of the problems that has always faced astronomers is the seemingly endless calculation that is needed to pinpoint the true positions of the stars and the planets. In 1614 John Napier (1550-1617), Laird of Merchiston in Scotland, published the first full set of logarithmic tables. In 1617 he invented a series of rods engraved with numbers in such a way that they could be set side by side and used for doing complex multiplications and divisions. The rods, usually made of ivory or bone, were soon known as "Napier's bones."

Rods marked with Napier's numbers

FAMILY LOYALTY

Caroline Herschel (1750-1848) was astronomical assistant and housekeeper to her brother, the great observational astronomer Sir William Herschel (p. 54). While he was busy grinding mirrors – a delicate task that could take up to 16 hours – Caroline would spoon-feed him as he worked to keep up his strength. As an astronomer of note in her own right, she discovered eight comets and was an influence on her brilliant nephew John (1792-1871), who became famous for his survey of the southern hemisphere.

Turning pegs

Number display

Handle

ASTRONOMICAL CALCULATOR

In the 19th century instrument makers began to construct mechanical calculators for complex, often repetitive, mathematical functions. With one turn of the handle, this calculator can produce a figure with up to 42 places.

Lantern

Barometer

Arm rest

Adjustable back

THE ASTRONOMICAL CHAIR

The astronomical chair is quite a late invention. When astronomers worked with big mural quadrants (p. 25), they needed a pair of steps to run up and down in order to reach the eyepiece of the telescope. It was not until the invention of the transit instrument in the late 17th century that astronomers could lie back and look at the stars. Chairs with padding on them did not appear for another 50 years.

Seat

KEEPING WARM

Being an astronomer was not a glamorous life. Before the advent of the camera, the job involved spending long hours in a roofless observatory, peering through an eyepiece at the stars, and making copious notes of observations. Suitable warm clothing would have been essential.

Ratchet for altering height of seat

Ratchet pin

Wheeled base

29

Spectroscopy

ASTRONOMERS HAVE BEEN ABLE to study the chemical composition of the stars and how hot they are for more than a century by means of spectroscopy. A spectroscope breaks down the "white" light coming from a celestial body into an extremely detailed spectrum. Working on Isaac Newton's discovery of the spectrum (p. 21), a German optician, Josef Fraunhofer (1787-1826), examined the spectrum created by light coming from the Sun and noticed a number of dark lines crossing it. In 1859 another German, Gustav Kirchhoff (1824-1887), discovered the significance of Fraunhofer's lines. They are produced by chemicals in the cooler, upper layers of the Sun (or a star) absorbing light. Each chemical has its own pattern of lines, like a fingerprint. By looking at the spectrum of the Sun, astronomers have found all the elements that are known on the Earth in the Sun's atmosphere.

THE COLORS OF THE RAINBOW
A rainbow is formed by the Sun shining through raindrops. The light is refracted by droplets of water as if each one were a prism.

Prism splits the light into its colors

The spectrum

Infrared band

Red

Rays of white light

Sodium lamp

Violet

The spectroscope would be mounted on a telescope here

HERSCHEL DISCOVERS INFRARED
In 1800 Sir William Herschel (p. 54) set up a number of experiments to test the relationship between heat and light. He repeated Newton's experiment of splitting white light into a spectrum (p. 21) and, by masking all the colors but one, was able to measure the individual temperatures of each color in the spectrum. He discovered that the red end of the spectrum is hotter than the violet end, but was surprised to note that an area where he could see no color, next to the red end of the spectrum, is much hotter than the rest of the spectrum. He called this area infrared, or "below the red."

Stand for photographic plate

Diffraction grating

Solar spectrum showing absorption lines

Sodium

Emission spectrum of sodium

Sodium

Spectroscope

LOOKING AT SODIUM
Viewing burning sodium in a flame through a spectroscope can help explain how spectroscopy works in space. According to Gustav Kirchhoff's first law of spectral analysis, a hot dense gas at high pressure produces a continuous spectrum of all colors. His second law states that a hot rarefied gas at low pressure produces an emission line spectrum, that is, a spectrum of bright lines against a dark background. His third law states that when light from a hot dense gas passes through a cooler gas before it is viewed, it produces an absorption line spectrum – a bright spectrum riddled with a number of dark, fine lines.

WHAT IS IN THE SUN?
When a sodium flame is viewed through a spectroscope (left), the emission spectrum produces the characteristic bright yellow lines (above). The section of the Sun's spectrum (top) shows a number of tiny "gaps" or dark lines. These are the Fraunhofer lines from which the chemical composition of the Sun can be determined. The two dark lines in the yellow part of the spectrum correspond to the sodium. As there is no sodium in the Earth's atmosphere, it must be coming from the Sun.

KIRCHHOFF AND BUNSEN

Following the invention of the clean-flame burner by the German chemist Robert Bunsen (1811-1899), it was possible to study the effect of different chemical vapors on the known pattern of spectral lines. Together, Gustav Kirchhoff and Bunsen invented a new instrument called the spectroscope to measure these effects. Within a few years, they had managed to isolate the spectra for many known substances, as well as discovering a few unknown elements.

Continuous spectrum

ABSORBING COLOR

To prove his laws of spectral analysis, Kirchhoff used sodium gas to show that when white light is directed through the gas, the characteristic color of the sodium is absorbed and the spectrum shows black lines where the sodium should have appeared. In the experiment shown above, a continuous spectrum (top) is produced by shining white light through a lens. When a petri dish of the chemical potassium permanganate in solution is placed between the lens and the light, some of the color of the spectrum is absorbed.

The spectrum of potassium permanganate

SPECTRUM OF THE STARS

By closely examining the spectral lines in the light received from a distant star, the astronomer can detect these "fingerprints" and uncover the chemical composition of the object being viewed. Furthermore, the heat of the source can also be discovered by studying the spectral lines. Temperature can be measured by the intensities of individual lines in their spectra. The width of the line provides information about temperature, movement, and presence of magnetic fields. With magnification, each of these spectra can be analyzed in more detail.

Eyepiece

Latticework frame

Prisms

Micrometer (p. 25)

Eyepiece

THE SPECTROSCOPE

A spectroscope uses a series of prisms or a diffraction grating – a device that diffracts light through fine lines to form a spectrum – to split light into its constituent wavelengths (pp. 32-33). Before the era of photography, an astronomer would view the spectrum produced with the eye, but now it is mostly recorded with an electronic detector called a CCD (p. 37). This 19th-century spectroscope uses a prism to split the light.

NORMAN LOCKYER (1836-1920)

During the solar eclipse of 1868, a number of astronomers picked up a new spectral line in the upper surface of the Sun, the chromosphere (p. 39). The English astronomer Lockyer realized that the line did not coincide with any of the known elements. The newly discovered element was named helium (*helios* is Greek for the sun god). Finally, in 1895, helium was found to be present on the Earth.

The radio telescope

WITH THE DISCOVERY OF non-visible light, such as infrared (p. 30), and electromagnetic and X-ray radiations, scientists began to wonder if objects in space might emit invisible radiation as well. The first such radiation to be discovered (by accident) was radio waves – the longest wavelengths of the electromagnetic spectrum. To detect radio waves, astronomers constructed huge dishes in order to capture the long waves and "see" detail. Even so, early radio telescopes were never large enough, proportionally, to catch the fine features that optical telescopes could resolve. Today, by electronically combining the output from many radio telescopes, a dish the size of the Earth can be synthesized, revealing details many times finer than optical telescopes. Astronomers routinely study all radiations from objects in space, often using detectors high above the Earth's atmosphere (p. 7).

ANDERS ÅNGSTRÖM (1814-1874)
Ångström was a Swedish astronomer who mapped the Fraunhofer lines in the Sun's spectrum (p. 30). The units needed to measure the wavelengths of the colors corresponding to these lines were so short that Ångström had to invent a new unit of length. The Ångström (symbol Å) is 10^{-10} meters.

Space telescope   Optical telescope   Optical telescope   Radio receiver

Gamma rays | Ultraviolet | Infrared | Standard broadcast
X-rays   Visible light   Microwaves | Long radio waves

ELECTROMAGNETIC SPECTRUM
The range of frequencies of electromagnetic radiation is known as the electromagnetic spectrum. Very low on the scale are radio waves, rising to infrared (p. 30), visible light, ultraviolet, and X-rays, with gamma rays at the highest frequency end of the spectrum. The radiations that pass through the Earth's atmosphere are light and radio waves, though infrared penetrates to the highest mountaintops. The remainder can only be detected by sending instruments into space in special probes (pp. 34-35). All telescopes – radio, optical, and infrared – "see" different aspects of the sky caused by the different physical processes going on.

EVIDENCE OF RADIO RADIATION
The first evidence of radio radiation coming from outer space was collected by the American scientist Karl Jansky (1905-1950) who, in 1931, using homemade equipment (above), investigated the static affecting short-wavelength radio-telephone communication. He deduced that this static must be coming from the center of our galaxy (pp. 62-63).

AMATEUR ASTRONOMER
On hearing about Jansky's discoveries, American amateur astronomer Grote Reber (1911-) built a large, moveable radio receiver in his backyard in 1936. It had a parabolic surface to collect the radio waves. With this 29-ft (9-m) dish, he began to map the radio emissions coming from the Milky Way. For years Reber was the only radio astronomer in the world.

ARECIBO RECEIVER
The mammoth Arecibo radio receiver is built in a natural limestone concavity in the jungle south of Arecibo, Puerto Rico. The "dish," which is a huge web of steel mesh, measures 1,000 ft (305 m) across, providing a 50-acre (20-hectare) collecting surface. Although the dish is fixed, overhead antennas can be moved to different parts of the sky.

HOT SPOTS

Radio astronomers can create temperature maps of planets. This false-color map shows temperatures just below Mercury's surface. Because Mercury is so close to the Sun, the hottest area is on Mercury's equator, shown here as red. The blue areas are the coolest.

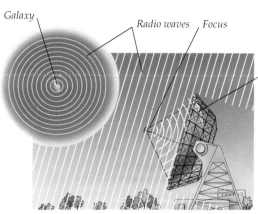

Galaxy

Radio waves   *Focus*

Parabolic dish

BERNARD LOVELL

English astronomer Bernard Lovell (1913-) was a pioneer of radio astronomy. He developed a research station at Jodrell Bank, England, in 1945 using surplus army radar equipment. He is seen here in the control room of the 250-ft- (76-m-) diameter Mark 1 radio telescope (later renamed the Lovell Telescope in his honor). The telescope's giant dish was commissioned in 1957.

HIGH-TECH TELESCOPE

Communications technology allows astronomers to work nearly anywhere in the world. All they need is a computer linkup. While optical telescopes are sited far from built-up areas (p. 27), clear skies are not necessary for radio astronomy. This telescope is the world's largest, fully steerable, single-dish radio telescope; it is 330 ft (100 m) in diameter and is located near Bonn, Germany.

HOW A RADIO TELESCOPE WORKS

The parabolic dish of a radio telescope can be steered to pick up radio signals. It focuses them to a point from which they are sent to a receiver, a recorder, and then a data room at a control center. Computer equipment then converts intensities of the incoming radio waves into images that are recognizable to our eyes as objects from space (p. 57).

THE VERY LARGE ARRAY

Scientists soon realized that radio telescopes could be connected together by electrical wires to form very large receiving surfaces. For example, two dishes 62 miles (100 km) apart can be linked electronically so that their receiving area is the equivalent of a 62-mile (100-km)-wide dish. One of the largest arrangements of telescopes is the Very Large Array (VLA) set up in the desert near Socorro, New Mexico. Twenty-seven parabolic dishes have been arranged in a huge "Y," covering more than 17 miles (27 km).

Parabolic dish

Mounting support

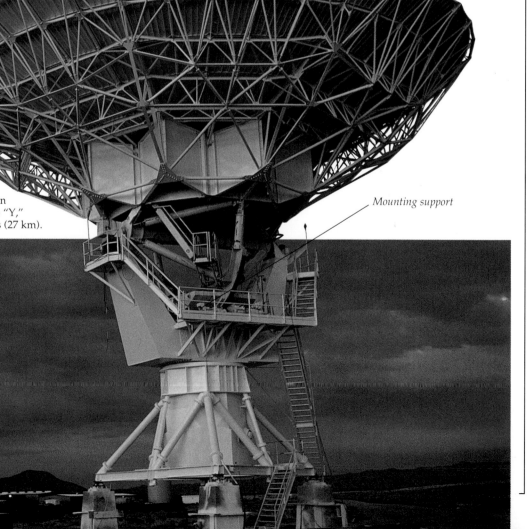

Venturing into space

FOLLOWING THE *APOLLO* MISSIONS, there has been no drive to return to the Moon. There is also little support for a mission that would send humans to Mars. As technology has improved, it makes more sense to use satellites and probes to send back information – this minimizes the risk to human life. The space race is over, but not our investigation of space. Instead of competing, countries share the costs of exploration, recognizing the huge benefits that space technology brings to our lives. The development of new, lightweight, yet strong, materials and water purification methods are direct spinoffs of space research. TV channels now rely on orbiting communications satellites. Ships, planes, and even cars navigate using satellite signals. Military satellites are used in early-warning systems. Our weather forecasts use images from meteorological satellites, while resources satellites monitor the Earth's surface.

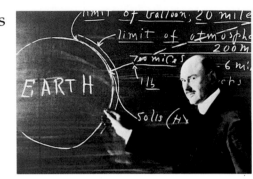

GETTING INTO SPACE
The American physicist Robert Goddard (1882-1945) launched the first liquid-fueled rocket in 1926. This fuel system overcame the major obstacle to launching an orbiting satellite, which was the weight of solid fuels. If a rocket is to reach a speed great enough to escape the Earth's gravitational field, it needs a thrust greater than the weight it is carrying.

LUNAR PROBES
The former USSR launched *Sputnik 1*, the first artificial satellite, into space in 1957. Between the late 1950s and 1976, several probes were sent to explore the surface of the Moon. *Luna 1* was the first successful lunar probe. It passed within 3,730 miles (6,000 km) of the Moon. *Luna 3* was the first probe to send back pictures to the Earth of the far side of the Moon (pp. 40-41). The first to achieve a soft landing was *Luna 9* in February 1966. *Luna 16* collected soil samples, bringing them back without any human involvement. The success of these missions forced people to take space exploration more seriously.

Luna 1

THE FIRST MAN IN SPACE
On April 12, 1961 the former USSR (now Russia) launched the 5-ton spaceship *Vostok 1*. It was manned by cosmonaut Yuri Gagarin (1934-1968), who made a complete circuit of the Earth at a height of 188 miles (303 km). He remained in space for 1 hour 29 minutes before landing back safely in the USSR. He was hailed as a national hero and is seen here being lauded by the Premier of the USSR, Nikita Khrushchev.

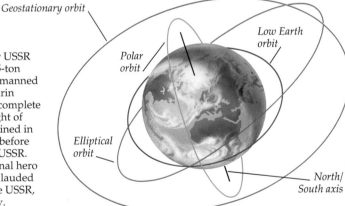

Geostationary orbit

Low Earth orbit

Polar orbit

Elliptical orbit

North/ South axis

SATELLITE ORBITS
A satellite is sent into an orbit that is most suitable for the kind of work it has to do. Space telescopes such as Hubble (p. 7) take the low orbits – 373 miles (600 km) above the Earth's surface. US spy and surveillance satellites orbit on a north/south axis to get a view of the whole Earth, while those belonging to Russia often follow elliptical orbits that allow them to spend more time over their own territory. Communications and weather satellites are positioned above the equator. They take exactly 24 hours to complete an orbit, and therefore seem to hover above the same point on the Earth's surface – known as a geostationary orbit.

LUNAR LANDING
Between 1969 and 1972, six crewed lunar landings took place. The first astronaut to set foot on the Moon was Neil Armstrong (1930-) on July 21, 1969. Scientifically, one of the major reasons for Moon landings was to try to understand the origin of the Moon itself and to understand its history and evolution. This photograph shows American astronaut James Irwin with the *Apollo 15* Lunar Rover in 1971.

COOPERATION IN SPACE

The European Space Agency's rocket, *Ariane*, is used by a number of European countries to launch a series of communications satellites. The satellite or probe that is carried into space is known as a payload. The idea of cooperation in space is markedly different from the 1960s and 1970s, when the U.S. and the USSR competed against each other. *Ariane* provides the means by which a group of less wealthy countries can band together and share the benefits of space-age technology. This photograph shows *Ariane 3* taking off from French Guiana in 1984. Unfortunately the rocket crashed shortly after this photograph was taken.

External fuel tank

The Space Shuttle

Launching satellites by rocket is expensive and wasteful because the launch vehicle is destroyed in the process. The U.S. Space Shuttle has proved to be a reusable alternative. Its missions last about a week and have included taking astronauts to the Hubble space telescope for repairs and carrying modules into space for the construction of a new space station.

THE SPACE SHUTTLE

The Shuttle is boosted into space by two huge, reusable solid-fuel booster rockets. They are jettisoned and then fall back to the Earth slowed by parachutes so they can be retrieved. The Shuttle returns to the Earth and lands at about 217 mph (350 km/h). It is protected from the intense heat of reentry by a shell of thermal tiles.

LIVING IN SPACE

The former USSR launched the first module of the *Mir* space station in 1986. The station had central living quarters surrounded by a series of docking ports. These could be used to expand the station – by adding more modules – or as entry points for cargo and supply ferries from Earth. The longest stay on *Mir* was by Dr. Valery Poliakov, who spent 438 days there. Scientists are still researching the effects on humans of prolonged periods in space.

BENEFITS OF SPACE PROBES

Meteorological satellites can monitor the changing patterns of the weather and plot ocean currents, which play a major role in determining the Earth's climate. Data gathered by monitoring such vast expanses as this Russian ice floe can be used to predict climate change. Resource satellites are used for geological and ecological research. For example, they map the distribution of plankton – a major part of the food chain – in ocean waters.

UNDERWATER TRAINING

In space, astronauts experience weightlessness, or zero gravity. This is not an easy thing to simulate on the Earth. The closest approximation is to train astronauts underwater to move and operate machinery. Even then the effect of resistance in water gives a false impression.

Felt protects parts where heat does not exceed 700°F (370°C)

United States

Solid-fuel rocket booster

Shuttle orbiter

The Solar System

THE SOLAR SYSTEM is the group of planets, moons, and space debris orbiting around our Sun. It is held together by the gravitational pull of the Sun, which is nearly 1,000 times more massive than all the planets put together. The Solar System was probably formed from a huge cloud of interstellar gas and dust that contracted under the force of its own gravity five billion years ago. The planets are divided into two groups. The four planets closest to the Sun are called "terrestrial" from the Latin word *terra* meaning "land" because they are small and dense and have hard surfaces. Four of the outer planets beyond Mars are called "Jovian" because they all resemble Jupiter – Jove was another name for the Roman god, Jupiter. These outer planets are largely made up of gases. Between Mars and Jupiter there is a zone of space debris – the asteroid belt (p. 58).

THE SECRET OF ASTRONOMY
This allegorical engraving shows Astronomy, with her star-covered robe, globe, telescope, and quadrant, next to a female figure who might represent Mathematics. The small angel between them holds a banner proclaiming *pondere et mensura*: "to weigh and measure" – which is the secret of the art of astronomy.

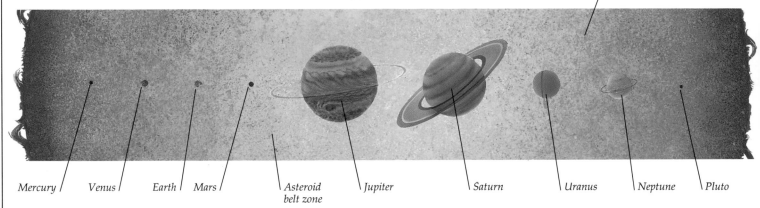

Sun

Mercury | Venus | Earth | Mars | Asteroid belt zone | Jupiter | Saturn | Uranus | Neptune | Pluto

RELATIVE SIZE
The Sun has a diameter of approximately 865,000 miles (1,392,000 km). It is almost 10 times larger than the largest planet, Jupiter, which is itself big enough to contain all the other planets put together. The planets are shown here to scale against the Sun. Those planets with orbits inside the Earth are sometimes referred to as the inferior planets; those beyond the Earth are the superior planets. The four small planets that orbit the Sun relatively closely – Mercury, Venus, Earth, and Mars – have lower masses than those of the next four, but have much greater densities (p. 45). Jupiter, Saturn, Uranus, and Neptune have large masses with low densities. They are more widely spaced apart and travel at great distances from the Sun. Pluto is the smallest planet in the Solar System and is in a category of its own (p. 57).

Saturn and eight moons

Neptune and one moon

Venus

Moon

Earth

Mercury

Sun

Mars and two moons

Jupiter and nine moons

Uranus and four moons

Turning handle

Gearing mechanism

TEACHING ASTRONOMY
During the 19th century, the astronomy of the Solar System was taught by mechanical instruments such as this orrery. The complex gearing of the machine is operated by a crank handle, which ensures that each planet completes its solar orbit relative to the other planets. The planets are roughly to a scale of 50,000 miles (80,500 km) to 1 in (3 cm), but the Sun would need to be 17 in (43 cm) in diameter for the model to be accurate.

CELESTIAL MECHANICS
The Frenchman Pierre Simon Laplace (1749-1827) was the first scientist to make an attempt to compute all the motions of the Moon and the planets by mathematical means. In his five-volume work, *Traité de méchanique céleste* (1799-1825), Laplace treated all motion in the Solar System as a purely mathematical problem, using his work to support the theory of universal gravitation (p. 21). His idea, for which he was severely criticized during the following century, was that the heavens were a great celestial machine, like a timepiece that, once set in motion, would go on forever.

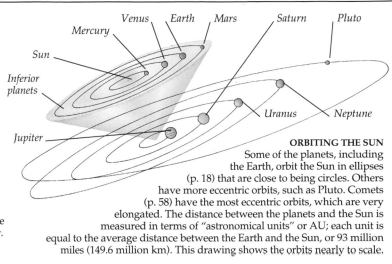

ORBITING THE SUN
Some of the planets, including the Earth, orbit the Sun in ellipses (p. 18) that are close to being circles. Others have more eccentric orbits, such as Pluto. Comets (p. 58) have the most eccentric orbits, which are very elongated. The distance between the planets and the Sun is measured in terms of "astronomical units" or AU; each unit is equal to the average distance between the Earth and the Sun, or 93 million miles (149.6 million km). This drawing shows the orbits nearly to scale.

Photographing the planets

One of the key tasks of space probes (pp. 34-35) is to send back pictures of distant planets and moons. They do this using imaging devices very similar to those used in digital cameras. The heart of the system is a CCD, or charge-coupled device. This is a silicon chip with thousands of light-sensitive pixels, or picture elements. The amount of light falling on each pixel produces a different electrical signal. This is read by an onboard computer and converted into a stream of digital signals that can be radioed back to Earth, where they are reconstructed into the image by computer.

Mariner 9 photographs of the surface of Mars

Escaping elements

Lighter elements

By increasing the vibration, the balls are given more energy

Heavier elements

Kinetic energy machine

CREATING COLOR
The CCDs used in astronomy rarely produce color images directly, but use the most sensitive black-and-white chips. To get a color image, three separate images are taken through color filters, and the results are combined in a computer to give a realistic color view.

HYDROGEN IN THE SOLAR SYSTEM
Hydrogen is a common element in the Solar System. Hydrogen atoms are so energetic that lightweight planets cannot hang on to them. This is why the heavier nitrogen makes up such a high percentage of the Earth's atmosphere (p. 42). Lighter hydrogen has escaped because the Earth's gravity is not strong enough to hold on to it. The red balls in this kinetic energy machine represent the heavier elements; the tiny silver balls represent the lighter elements, such as hydrogen. Our massive Sun is made up largely of hydrogen. Its great mass pulls the hydrogen inward, and, at its core, hydrogen fuses into helium under the extreme heat and pressure. It is this reaction, like a giant hydrogen bomb, that makes the Sun shine. Hydrogen also makes up a large part of Jupiter, Saturn, Uranus, and Neptune (pp. 50-57).

COLOR MOSAIC OF MARS
The detail in an individual CCD image of a planet is limited by the number of pixels on the chip. To get a high-quality image, several shots are taken of different parts of the planet, and then a mosaic is produced, like this one of Mars.

The Sun

ALMOST EVERY ANCIENT CULTURE recognized the Sun as the giver of life and primary power behind events here on the Earth. The Sun is the center of our Solar System, our local star. It has no permanent features because it is gaseous – mainly incandescent hydrogen. Since it is so close, astronomers study the Sun in order to understand the nature of the stars in general. They focus mostly on the layers of atmosphere that extend out into space – the corona, the chromosphere, and the photosphere. By using spectroscopic analysis (pp. 30-31), scientists know that the Sun, like most stars (pp. 60-61), is made up mostly of hydrogen. In its core, the hydrogen nuclei are so compressed that they eventually fuse into helium. This is the same thing that happens in a hydrogen atomic bomb. Every minute, the Sun converts 240 million tons of mass into energy. Albert Einstein's famous formula, $E=mc^2$, shows how mass and energy are mutually interchangeable (p. 63), helping scientists understand the source of the Sun's energy.

THE CORONAGRAPH
In 1930 the French astronomer Bernard Lyot (1897-1952) invented the coronagraph. It allows the Sun's corona to be viewed without waiting for a total solar eclipse.

VIEWING THE SUN
Even though the Sun is more than 92 million miles (149 million km) from the Earth, its rays are still bright enough to damage the eyes permanently. The Sun should *never* be viewed directly, and certainly not through a telescope or binoculars. Galileo went blind looking at the Sun. This astronomer is at the Kitt Peak National Observatory in Arizona. Two mirrors at the top of the solar telescope tower reflect the Sun's image down a tube to the mirror below. Inside the tube there is a vacuum. This prevents distortion that would be caused by the air in the tower.

THE DIPLEIDOSCOPE
Local noon occurs when the Sun crosses the local north/south meridian (p. 27). In the 19th century, a more accurate device than the gnomon (p. 14) was sought to indicate when noon occurred. The dipleidoscope, invented in 1842, is an instrument with a hollow, right-angled prism, which has two silvered sides and one clear side. As the Sun passes directly overhead, the two reflected images are resolved into a single one. This shows when it is local noon.

Earth's axis

Southern hemisphere tilted toward the Sun

Summer in Australia

CHANGING SEASONS
The seasons change because the Earth rotates on a north/south axis (p. 12) as it orbits the Sun. The axis is tilted at an angle of 23½°. When the South Pole is tilted toward the Sun, the southern hemisphere experiences summer and the northern hemisphere winter. The path of the Sun across the sky also changes because of this tilt. It is lower in winter, and the days are shorter, and higher in the summer when the days are longer. Countries close to the equator do not have such extremes of temperature or changes in the length of day.

Hour dial

Prominence

Eyepiece

Prism container

Leveling tube

Compass

Chromosphere

Photosphere

THE CORONA

The outermost layer of the Sun's atmosphere is called the corona. Even though it extends millions of miles into space, it cannot be seen during the day because of the brightness of the blue sky. During a total eclipse, the corona appears like a crown around the Moon. It is clearly seen in this picture of a total eclipse over Mexico in March 1970.

Corona

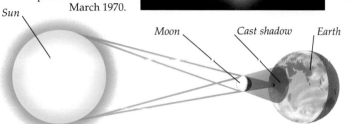

Sun *Moon* *Cast shadow* *Earth*

SOLAR ECLIPSE

A solar eclipse happens when a new Moon passes directly between the Earth and the Sun, casting a shadow on the surface of the Earth. From an earthly perspective, it looks as if the Moon has blocked out the light of the Sun. Total eclipses of the Sun are very rare in any given location, occurring roughly once every 360 years in the same place. However, several solar eclipses may occur each year.

Sunspots

Sunspots are cooler areas on the Sun's surface, where the magnetic field has disturbed the passage of heat from the core to its photosphere. When sunspots are at a maximum, the Sun also experiences large explosive eruptions called flares. These flares blast large numbers of charged particles into space. If these particles reach the Earth, they can cause disruption in radio communications and the wonderful effects of the aurora borealis and aurora australis.

PLOTTING THE SUNSPOTS

By observing the changing position of sunspots, we can see that the Sun is spinning. Unlike the planets, however, the whole mass of the Sun does not spin at the same rate because it is not solid. The Sun's equator takes 25 Earth days to make one complete rotation. The Sun's poles take nearly 30 days to accomplish the same task. These photographs are a record of the movements of a large spot group on 14 days in March/April 1947.

A PHOTOHELIOGRAPH

Astronomers watch sunspots through an adapted telescope. Instead of an eyepiece, there is a large screen of filtered glass. The Sun's image is projected onto the glass, which is marked with coordinates. The astronomer can count and measure sunspots without looking directly at the Sun.

SOLAR ATMOSPHERE

Since the Sun is a star, it does not have a surface. It has layers of gases of different densities. Most of the visible light of the Sun comes from the photosphere, which is about 190-250 miles (300-400 km) thick. The next layer out is the chromosphere, which is hotter than the photosphere. The outer layer is called the corona. Since the Sun is in a constantly volatile state, its layers are always subject to disturbance. Prominences – huge eruptions from the corona that extend outward for tens of thousands of miles – are directly related to disturbances of the Sun's magnetic field.

FACTS ABOUT THE SUN

Prominence
Photosphere
Radioactive core
Radiative zone
Convective zone

- **Equatorial diameter** 0.86 million miles/1.4 million km
- **Distance from the Earth** 93 million miles/ 149 million km
- **Rotational period** 25 Earth days
- **Volume** (Earth =1) 1,306,000
- **Mass** (Earth =1) 333,000
- **Density** (water = 1) 1.41
- **Temperature at surface** 10,000°F

The Moon

EARLY MOON MAP
The same side of the Moon always faces toward the Earth. Because the Moon's orbit is not circular and it travels at different speeds, we can see more than half of the Moon. This phenomenon, called libration, means that about 59 percent of the Moon's surface is visible from the Earth. In 1647 Johannes Hevelius (1611-1687) published his lunar atlas *Selenographia* showing the Moon's librations.

THE MOON IS THE EARTH'S only satellite, averaging about 239,000 miles (384,000 km) away. Next to the Sun it is the brightest object in our sky, more than 2,000 times as bright as Venus. The origin of the Moon is still the subject of heated debate. Some scientists believe that the Earth and the Moon were formed at the same time from the dust and gas of the primordial Solar System. Others argue that the Moon was a body passing the Earth that got caught by the Earth's gravitational field. Some think that a body the size of Mars once collided with the Earth. The impact splashed debris into space, some of which eventually formed the Moon.

Shadow is used to calculate the height of crater walls

COPERNICUS CRATER
The Moon's craters were formed between 3.5 and 4.5 billion years ago by the impact of countless meteorites. These impact craters are all named after famous astronomers and philosophers. Because the Moon has no atmosphere, there has been little erosion of its surface. This plaster model shows Copernicus crater, which is 56 miles (90 km) across and 11,000 ft (3,352 m) deep. Inside the crater there are mountains with peaks 8 miles (5 km) above the crater's floor.

Floor of the crater

Crater walls

Umbra or total shadow

Sun

Moon's orbit

Earth

Moon

Penumbra, or partial shadow

A LUNAR ECLIPSE
An eclipse happens when the Earth passes directly between the Sun and the full Moon, so that the Earth's shadow falls on to the surface of the Moon. This obscures the Moon for the duration of the eclipse.

Lunar equator

Equatorial dial

Tide tables   *Compass*   *Latitude tables*

TIDE TABLES
The pull of the Moon's gravity (p. 21), and to a lesser extent, the Sun's, causes the water of the seas on the Earth to rise and fall. This effect is called a tide. When the Sun, the Moon, and the Earth are all aligned at a new or full moon, the tidal "pull" is the greatest. These are called spring tides. When the Sun and the Moon are at right angles to each other, they produce smaller pulls called neap tides. This compendium (1569) contains plates with tables indicating the tides of some European cities. It was an essential instrument for sailors entering harbor.

PHASES OF THE MOON

The phases of the Moon are caused by the constantly changing series of angles formed by the Sun and the Moon as the Moon revolves around the Earth. When the Moon and the Sun are on opposite sides of the Earth, the Sun shines directly on the Moon's surface, resulting in a Full Moon. When the area of the lit surface increases, the Moon is said to be waxing; as it decreases, it is said to be waning.

Waxing crescent Moon at 4 days

Full Moon at 14 days

Waning 19-day Moon

Moon at 21 days

Moon at 24 days

Gearing

Meridian circle

THE SURFACE OF THE MOON

The features on the far side of the Moon were a mystery until the late 1950s. This view of the terrain was taken by the *Apollo 11* lunar module in 1969. One of the primary purposes for exploring the Moon was to bring back samples of rock to study them and to discover their origins. The Moon is made up of similar but not identical material to that found on the Earth. There is less iron on the Moon, but the major minerals are silicates as they are on the Earth (p. 43) – though they are slightly different in composition. This has led to the latest theory about the Moon's origins, sometimes known as the "Big Splash" theory. The impact of a large planet tore away parts of the Earth and parts of the large planet to create the unique geological makeup of the Moon.

INVESTIGATING MOON ROCK

Rocks from the Moon have been investigated by geologists in the same way as they study Earth rocks. The rocks are ground down to thin slices and then looked at under a powerful microscope. The minerals, chiefly feldspar and olivine, which are abundant on the Earth, are unweathered. This is exceptional for geologists because there are no Earth rocks that are totally unweathered.

Cross polarized light in the microscope gives colors

Watery clearness shows no weathering

Hour circle

Earth

A MOON GLOBE

Selenography is the study of the surface features of the Moon and this selenograph, created by the artist John Russell in 1797, is a Moon globe. Only a little more than half of the globe is filled with images because at that time the features on the far side of the Moon were unknown. Not until the Russians received the earliest transmissions from the *Luna 3* probe in October 1959 was possible to see images of what was on the Moon's far side.

FACTS ABOUT THE MOON

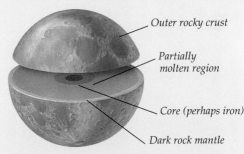

Outer rocky crust

Partially molten region

Core (perhaps iron)

Dark rock mantle

- **Interval between two New Moons** 29 days 12 hr 44 min
- **Temperature at surface** 230°F to 130°F
- **Rotational period** 27.3 Earth days
- **Mean distance from the Earth** 239,000 miles/384,000 km
- **Volume** (Earth = 1) 0.02
- **Mass** (Earth = 1) 0.012
- **Density** (water = 1) 3.34
- **Equatorial diameter** 2,160 miles/3,480 km

The Earth

THE EARTH IS THE ONLY PLANET in the Solar System that is capable of supporting advanced life. Its unique combination of liquid water, a rich oxygen- and nitrogen-based atmosphere, and dynamic weather patterns provides the basic elements for a diverse distribution of plant and animal life. Over millions of years, landforms and oceans have been constantly changing, mountains have been raised up and eroded away, and continental plates drift across the Earth. Some scientists see this harmonious balance being threatened by overpopulation by human beings. The stripping of rainforests and burning fossil fuels mean that carbon dioxide is building up in the atmosphere faster than plant life can recycle it back into oxygen. Since carbon dioxide traps the heat of the Sun beneath the Earth's atmosphere, but stops it from getting out again ("greenhouse effect," p. 47), the Earth's temperature may rise.

THE EARTH AND THE MOON
The English astronomer James Bradley (1693-1762) noted that many stars appear to have irregularities in their paths. He deduced that this is due to the effect of observing from an Earth that wobbles on its axis, caused by the gravitational pull of the Moon (p. 41).

CONSTANT GEOGRAPHICAL CHANGE
The Earth's crust is made up of a number of plates that are constantly moving because of currents that rise and fall from the molten iron core at the center of the Earth. Where the plates collide, they can lift the rocky landscape upward to create mountain ranges that are then eroded into craggy shapes like the Andes in Patagonia. The tensions caused by these movements sometimes result in earthquakes and volcanic activity.

Sahara desert

Water covers two-thirds of the Earth's surface

Canada

Removable terrestrial globe

Constellation of the Great Bear

Celestial sphere

Case

North Pole

Cloud layers

POCKET GLOBE
A globe is a convenient tool for recording specific features of the Earth's surface. This 19th-century pocket globe summarizes the face of the world from the geopolitical perspective, where the continents are divided into nations and spheres of influence. On the inside of the case is a map of the celestial sphere (pp. 12-13), with all the constellations marked out.

Collenia

FOSSILIZED ALGAE
Dead plants and creatures buried in sediment are slowly turned to rock, becoming fossils. This rock contains the fossilized remains of tiny algae that were one of the earliest life forms.

HUMAN DAMAGE
Many scientists wonder if humans, like the dinosaurs, might also become extinct. The dinosaur seems to have been a passive victim of the changing Earth, while humans are playing a key role in the destruction of their environment. In the year 2000 there were more than 6 billion people on the Earth – all producing waste and pollution. In addition to global warming that may be occurring due to the greenhouse effect, chemicals are being released that deplete the ozone layer – a layer in the atmosphere that keeps out dangerous ultraviolet radiation.

EARLY LIFE ON THE EARTH
The first life on the Earth was primitive plants that took carbon dioxide from the air and released oxygen during photosynthesis. Animals evolved when there was enough oxygen in the atmosphere to sustain them. Knowledge about evolving life forms comes in the form of fossils in the rocks (left). However, life forms survive only if environmental conditions on the Earth are suitable for them. The dinosaurs, for example, though perfectly adapted to their age became extinct about 65 million years ago.

Plant-eating *Edmontosaurus*

LIFE-GIVING ATMOSPHERE
Our atmosphere extends out for about 600 miles (1,000 km). It sustains life and protects us from the harmful effects of solar radiation. It has several layers, but the life-sustaining layer is the troposphere, up to 6 miles (10 km) above the Earth's surface.

Carbon dioxide *Nitrogen*
Oxygen
4.5 Ma *Today*
Hydrogen

Magnetosphere shields the Earth from solar winds

Aurora

Meteor shower (p. 59)

Weather satellite

Ozone layer

Maximum height for a balloon

Maximum height for an airplane

Mount Everest

Troposphere

Clouds

EVOLUTION OF THE ATMOSPHERE
Since the Earth was formed, the chemical makeup of the atmosphere has evolved. Carbon dioxide (CO_2) decreased significantly between 4.5 billion and 3 billion years ago. There was a comparable rise in nitrogen. The levels of oxygen began to rise at the same time, due to photosynthesis by primitive plants, which used up CO_2 and released oxygen.

THE SPHERICAL EARTH
As early as the 5th century BC the Greek philosophers had proposed that the Earth is spherical; by the 3rd century BC, they had worked out a series of experiments to prove it. But it was not until the launching of the first satellites in the late 1950s that humans saw what their planet looks like from space. The one feature that makes the Earth unique is the great abundance of liquid water; more than two-thirds of the surface is covered with water. Water makes the Earth a dynamic place. Erosion, tides, weather patterns, and plentiful forms of life are all tied to the presence of water. There is more water in the Sahara Desert in North Africa than there is on all of Venus (pp. 46-47).

FACTS ABOUT THE EARTH

Oxygen/nitrogen atmosphere
Solid iron core
Molten iron core
Rocky mantle
Rocky crust

- **Sidereal period** 365.26 days
- **Temperature** –94°F to +130°F
- **Rotational period** 23 hr 56 min
- **Mean distance from the Sun** 93 million miles/ 150 million km
- **Volume** 1 • **Mass** 1
- **Density** (water = 1) 5.52
- **Equatorial diameter** 7,930 miles/12,760 km
- **Number of satellites** 1

Mercury

The planet Mercury is named after the Greco-Roman messenger of the gods, because it circles the Sun faster than the other planets, completing its circuit in 88 Earth days. Because it travels so close to the Sun, Mercury is often difficult to observe. Even though its reflected light makes it one of the brightest objects in the night sky, Mercury is never far enough from the Sun to be able to shine out brightly. It is only visible as a "morning" or "evening" star, hugging the horizon just before or after the Sun rises or sets. Like Venus, Mercury also has phases (p. 20). Being so close to the Sun, temperatures during the day on Mercury are hot enough to melt many metals. At night they drop to –279°F (–180°C), making the temperature range the greatest of all the planets. The gravitational pull of the Sun has "stolen" any atmosphere that Mercury had to protect itself against these extremes.

EARLY MERCURY MAP
Although many astronomers have tried to record the elusive face of Mercury, the most prolific observer was the French astronomer, Eugène Antoniadi (1870-1944). His maps, drawn between 1924 and 1929, show a number of huge valleys and deserts. Closeup views by the *Mariner 10* space probe uncovered an altogether different picture (below).

CRATERED TERRAIN
The surface of Mercury closely resembles our crater-covered Moon (p. 40). Mercury's craters were also formed by the impact of meteorites, and the lack of atmosphere has kept the landscape unchanged. Around the edges of the craters, a series of concentric ridges record how the surface was pushed outward by the force of the impact.

Caloris impact

Mountain range   *Seismic waves*

SEISMIC WAVES
Some of Mercury's hills and mountains were created by the impact of a huge meteorite (p. 59). The impact created a crater, known as Caloris Basin, where the meteorite struck the surface and sent out seismic, or shock, waves through the semi-molten core of the planet. These waves traveled through Mercury to the other side, where the crust buckled and mountain ranges were thrown up.

SURFACE OF MERCURY
This image is a mosaic of photographs taken during *Mariner 10*'s journey past Mercury in 1974. Mercury seems to have shrunk a bit after it was formed. This has caused a series of winding ridges, called scarps, that are unique to the planet. The entire surface is heavily cratered. The space probe *Mariner* also discovered that Mercury had a magnetic field about 1 percent the strength of the Earth's magnetic field.

OBSERVING MERCURY
In 1973 the *Mariner 10* space probe was sent into orbit around the Sun where it behaved rather like a mini-planet. It sent back images of Mercury on three separate encounters before its cameras failed.

LOOKING AT VOLUME

These blocks – wood, aluminum, and iron – all have the same volume, that is they occupy the same amount of space. Despite being the same size, however, these materials do not have the same mass and density, nor do they weigh the same. This is also true of the planets. For example, Mercury, though small, has a higher density than that of some of the larger planets.

Wood

Iron

Wood

Aluminum

Iron

Measuring planets

Whereas we can weigh and measure objects on the Earth, we have to figure out the space a planet occupies (volume), how much matter it contains (mass), and its density by looking at its behavior, by analyzing its gravitational pull on nearby objects, and by using data gained by space probes (pp. 34-35). Density is the mass for every unit of volume of an object (mass divided by the volume).

Saturn

Mercury

COMPARING DENSITY

Mercury has great mass for its size. Even though it is only slightly larger than the Earth's Moon, its mass is four times that of the Moon. This means its density must be nearly as high as the Earth's, most likely due to a very high quantity of iron. Astronomers believe that Mercury must have a massive iron core that takes up nearly a quarter of its radius to achieve such great mass – a fact backed up by *Mariner 10*'s evidence of a magnetic field. When the densities of Mercury and Saturn, the huge gas giant (pp. 52-53), are compared, Saturn would float and Mercury, whose density is seven times as great, would sink.

MEASURING MASS

Mass is how much matter an object contains. A beam balance can be used to find the mass of a material. Here a piece of wood and a piece of iron of identical proportions and volume are placed on the balance. The iron has the greater mass. By dividing the mass (measured in grams) of the wood and the iron by their volume (measured in cubic centimeters), it can be calculated that iron is a denser material than wood.

ORBITAL PERIOD

The tidal force of the Earth has locked its Moon into rotating so that one side of the Moon always faces the Earth (p. 40). This means the rotational period of the Moon equals its monthly period of revolution around the Earth. Since the orbit of Mercury is elongated, like an oval, it is locked into a rotational period where the planet spins 1½ times during each orbit of the Sun. This means that its year (how long it takes to orbit the Sun) is 88 Earth days, while its day (the time it takes to rotate – sunrise to sunrise) is 176 Earth days.

Moon

Earth

Mercury

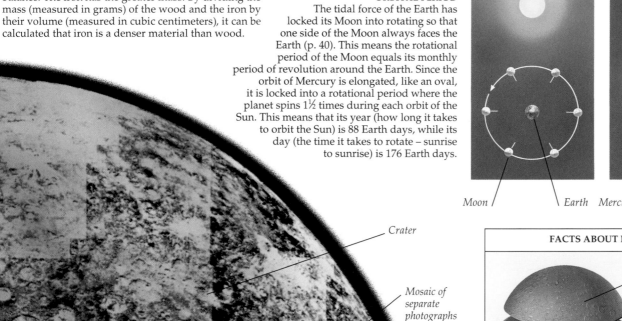

Crater

Mosaic of separate photographs

FACTS ABOUT MERCURY

Rocky crust

Iron and nickel core

Rocky mantle

Helium- and sodium-rich atmosphere

- **Sidereal period** 88 Earth days
- **Temperature at surface** −292°F to +800°F
- **Rotational period** 58.6 Earth days
- **Mean distance from the Sun** 36 million miles / 58 million km
- **Volume** (Earth = 1) 0.056 • **Mass** (Earth = 1) 0.055
- **Density** (water = 1) 5.43
- **Equatorial diameter** 3,030 miles / 4,880 km
- **Number of satellites** 0

Venus

PEOPLE OFTEN MISTAKE VENUS for a star. After the Moon, it is the brightest object in our night sky. Because it is so close in size to the Earth, until the 20th century astronomers assumed that it might be in some ways like the Earth. The probes sent to investigate have shown that this is not so. The dense cloudy atmosphere of Venus hides its surface from even the most powerful telescope. Only radar can penetrate to map the planet's features. Until it became possible to determine the surface features – largely flat, volcanic plains – scientists could not tell how long the Venusian day was. The atmosphere is deadly. It is made up of a mixture of carbon dioxide and sulfuric acid, which causes an extreme "greenhouse effect" in which heat is trapped by the lethal atmosphere. The ancients, however, saw only a beautifully bright planet and so they named it after their goddess of love. Nearly all the features mapped on the surface of Venus have been named after women, such as Pavlova, Sappho, and Phoebe.

VENUS IN THE NIGHT SKY
This photograph was taken from the Earth. It shows the crescent Moon with Venus in the upper left of the sky. Shining like a lantern at twilight, Venus looks so attractive that some astronomers were inspired to believe it must be a beautiful planet.

CALCULATING DISTANCES
One way to calculate the distance of the Earth from the Sun is for a number of observers all around the world to measure the transit of a planet (the passage of the planet as it crosses the disc of the Sun and appears in silhouette). The British explorer Captain James Cook led one of the many expeditions in 1769 to observe the Transit of Venus from Tahiti. Calculations made from these observations also enabled astronomers to work out the relative measurements of the entire Solar System.

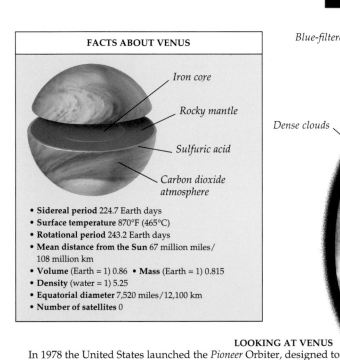

FACTS ABOUT VENUS

Iron core

Rocky mantle

Sulfuric acid

Carbon dioxide atmosphere

- **Sidereal period** 224.7 Earth days
- **Surface temperature** 870°F (465°C)
- **Rotational period** 243.2 Earth days
- **Mean distance from the Sun** 67 million miles/ 108 million km
- **Volume** (Earth = 1) 0.86 • **Mass** (Earth = 1) 0.815
- **Density** (water = 1) 5.25
- **Equatorial diameter** 7,520 miles/12,100 km
- **Number of satellites** 0

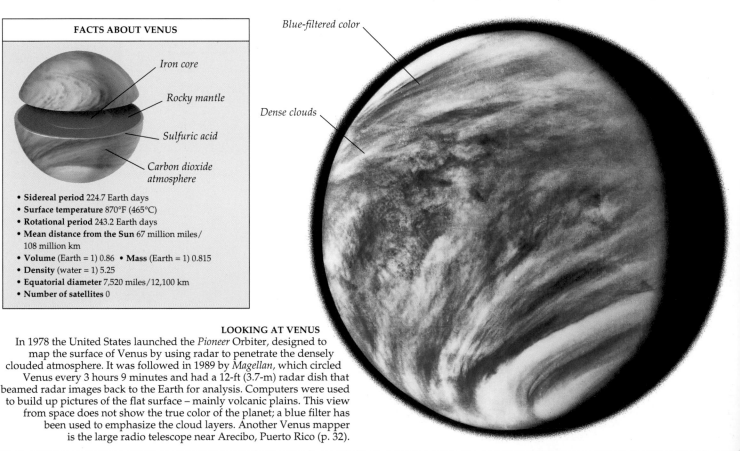

Blue-filtered color

Dense clouds

LOOKING AT VENUS
In 1978 the United States launched the *Pioneer* Orbiter, designed to map the surface of Venus by using radar to penetrate the densely clouded atmosphere. It was followed in 1989 by *Magellan*, which circled Venus every 3 hours 9 minutes and had a 12-ft (3.7-m) radar dish that beamed radar images back to the Earth for analysis. Computers were used to build up pictures of the flat surface – mainly volcanic plains. This view from space does not show the true color of the planet; a blue filter has been used to emphasize the cloud layers. Another Venus mapper is the large radio telescope near Arecibo, Puerto Rico (p. 32).

PUZZLING SURFACE

Even with the best telescope, Venus looks almost blank. This led Russian astronomer Mikhail Lomonosov (p. 28) to propose that the Venusian surface is densely covered with cloud. As recently as 1955, British astronomer Fred Hoyle (1915-2001) argued that the clouds are actually drops of oil and that the oceans on Venus are oceans of oil. Radar has shown that Venus's surface is actually covered with live volcanoes.

ASSEMBLING VENERA PROBES

During the 1960s and 1970s the former USSR sent a number of probes called *Venera* to investigate the surface of Venus. They were surprised when three of the probes stopped functioning as soon as they entered the Venusian atmosphere. Later *Venera* probes showed the reason why – the atmospheric pressure on the planet was 90 times that of Earth, the atmosphere itself was heavily acidic, and the temperature was 850°F (465°C).

Color balance

Feet of probe

Sunlight reflected

Carbon dioxide clouds let light through but no infrared out

Sulfuric acid layer

GREENHOUSE EFFECT

The great amount of carbon dioxide in Venus's atmosphere means that, while sunlight can penetrate, heat cannot escape. This has led to a runaway "greenhouse effect." Temperatures on the surface easily reach 900°F (465°C), even though the thick cloud layers keep out as much as 80 percent of the Sun's rays.

Volcanic activity

Infrared radiation

Sif Mons volcano

LANDING ON VENUS

This image was sent back by *Venera 13* when it landed on Venus in 1982. Part of the space probe can be seen bottom left and the color scale is in the lower middle of the picture. The landscape appears barren, made up of volcanic rocks. There was plenty of light for photography, but the spacecraft succumbed to the ovenlike conditions after only an hour.

Gula Mons volcano

Lava flows

THREE-DIMENSIONAL VIEW

This image of the Western Eistla Region, sent by *Magellan*, shows the volcanic lava flows (see here as the bright features) that cover the landscape and blanket the original Venusian features. Most of the landscape is covered by shallow craters. The simulated colors are based on those recorded by the Soviet *Venera* probes.

Mars

MARS APPEARS PALE ORANGE IN THE NIGHT SKY. The Babylonians, Greeks, and Romans all named it after their gods of war. In reality, Mars is a small planet – only half the size of the Earth – but there are similarities. Mars, like the Earth, has a 24-hour day, polar caps, and an atmosphere. Not surprisingly, Mars has always been the most popular candidate as a site for possible extraterrestrial life. Many scientists believe that some form of life – or at least evidence of past life – may remain within the planet, but no life could survive on the surface. The atmosphere is too thin to block out deadly ultraviolet rays. Mars is also farther from the Sun than the Earth, making it a lot colder.

MARTIAN MARKINGS
In 1659, Dutch scientist Christiaan Huygens (1629-1695) drew the first map of Mars, showing a V-shaped mark on the surface that reappeared in the same place every 24 hours. This was Syrtis Major. He concluded, correctly, that its regular appearance indicated the length of the Martian day. American astronomer Percival Lowell (1855-1916) made a beautiful series of drawings of the Martian canals described by Schiaparelli (below). Closer inspections showed that these canals were optical illusions caused by the eye's connecting unrelated spots.

Arabia region

CANALS ON MARS
The Italian astronomer Giovanni Schiaparelli (1835-1910) made a close study of the surface of Mars. In 1877 he noticed a series of dark lines that seemed to form some sort of network. Schiaparelli called them *canali,* translated as "channels" or "canals." This optical illusion seems to be the origin of the myth that Mars is occupied by a sophisticated race of hydraulic engineers. It was Eugène Antoniadi (p. 44) who made the first accurate map of Mars.

Ice cliff

Ice cap

AROUND THE PLANET MARS
The Martian atmosphere is much thinner than that of the Earth and is composed mostly of carbon dioxide. The *Viking 2* space probe recorded a noticeable amount of water vapor and ice cliffs (right), and photographs taken by the first orbiting space probe, *Mariner 9,* showed a series of winding valleys in the Chryse region that could have been dried-up river beds. Mars also has large volcanoes. One of them – Olympus Mons – is the largest in the Solar System. There are also deserts, canyons, and polar ice caps.

Computer-processed view of Mars from *Viking* orbiters (1980)

EVIDENCE OF POLAR ICE
In 2001 and 2002, *Mars Odyssey* showed that there are large ice reserves beneath much of the Martian soil. The planet has white markings covering both poles that seem to shrink and expand like our polar caps on the Earth. The Martian ice caps are largely composed of water ice and some frozen carbon dioxide. The ice cliffs shown here are up to 2 miles (3.5 km) thick.

Robotic arm

SAMPLING ROCK

In 1997, *Pathfinder* landed on Mars with the 25-in- (63-cm-) long *Sojourner* robot rover. The rover carried special instruments so that it could analyze the composition of Martian rocks.

TESTING FOR LIFE

The two *Viking* probes in the 1970s carried out simple experiments on Martian soil. They found no signs of life.

GLOBAL SURVEYOR

Mars Global Surveyor began orbiting Mars in 1997. *Surveyor* is studying the planet's weather and chemical makeup, as well as photographing and mapping its surface.

Assembling the *Viking* lander

DESERT LANDSCAPE

Mars resembles a desert. Winds whip up the red dust and it becomes suspended in the atmosphere, giving the sky a reddish hue. To make sure that the *Viking* images could be reproduced in their true colors, the spacecraft carried a series of color swatches (p. 47). Its photographs of these were corrected until the swatches were in their known colors, so the scientists could be confident that the landscape colors were also shown correctly.

MARTIAN MOONS

Mars has two small moons, Phobos (right) and Deimos, 17 and 10 miles (28 and 16 km) in diameter. Since the orbit of Deimos is only 14,580 miles (23,460 km) from the center of Mars, it will probably be pulled down to the surface with a crash in about 50 million years.

GULLIES ON MARS

Images sent back by *Mars Global Surveyor* show these intriguing marks. They are gullies on the wall of a meteor impact crater. It is possible that they formed when the permafrost beneath the surface melted, allowing groundwater up to the surface. They are the best evidence so far for water on Mars. The ripples at the bottom of the picture are sand dunes.

FACTS ABOUT MARS

Carbon dioxide atmosphere

Solid crust

Solid iron core

Rocky mantle

- **Sidereal period** 687 Earth days
- **Surface temperature** –185° to 75°F (118° to 25°C)
- **Rotational period** 24 hr 37 min
- **Mean distance from the Sun** 140 million miles/ 230 million km
- **Volume** (Earth=1) 0.15
- **Mass** (Earth=1) 0.11
- **Density** (water=1) 3.95
- **Equatorial diameter** 4,220 miles/6,790 km
- **Number of satellites** 2

Jupiter

THIS HUGE, BRIGHT PLANET is the largest world in our Solar System; four of its moons are the size of planets. It is different in structure from the solid inner planets. Most of Jupiter's bulk is gas – mainly hydrogen and helium. Below the level of the clouds, the pressure is so great that the hydrogen is compressed into its liquid form and, farther down, turns into metallic hydrogen. It emits more heat radiation than it receives from the Sun, because it continues shrinking at a rate of a fraction of an inch per year. Had Jupiter been many times more massive, the gas at its core would have been hot and dense enough for nuclear fusion reactions to take place (p. 38), and Jupiter would have become a star. Even though Jupiter has remained a planet, space probes, which take several years to get there, must be protected from Jupiter's fierce radiation belts. The *Galileo* spacecraft has been in orbit around Jupiter since 1995. It has transmitted some amazing photographs of Jupiter and its moons.

JUPITER'S RINGS
The US *Pioneer* missions were sent past Jupiter in the early 1970s, *Pioneer 10* sending back the first pictures. In 1977 the US sent two *Voyager* probes to explore Jupiter's cloud tops and five of its moons. *Voyager 1* uncovered a faint ring – like Saturn's rings (p. 53) – circling the planet. The thin yellow ring (approximately 18 miles/30 km thick) can be seen at the top of the photograph.

SEEING THE RED SPOT
In 1660 the English scientist Robert Hooke (1635-1702) reported seeing "a spot in the largest of the three belts of Jupiter." Gian Cassini (p. 28) saw the spot at the same time, but subsequent astronomers were unable to find it. The Great Red Spot was observed again in 1878 by the American astronomer Edward Barnard (1857-1923).

FACTS ABOUT JUPITER

- Atmosphere
- Rocky core
- Metallic hydrogen and helium
- Liquid hydrogen and helium

- **Sidereal period** 11.86 Earth years
- **Temperature at cloud tops** −240°F (−150°C)
- **Rotational period** 9 hr 55 min
- **Mean distance from the Sun** 484 million miles/ 778 million km
- **Volume** (Earth = 1) 1,319 • **Mass** (Earth = 1) 318
- **Density** (water = 1) 1.33
- **Equatorial diameter** 89,350 miles/142,980 km
- **Number of satellites** over 60

North Polar region
North Temperate Belt
North Tropical Zone
Storm system
Equatorial Belt
Equatorial Zone
South Tropical Zone
South Temperate Belt
Great Red Spot
South Polar region

JUPITER'S CLOUDS
The cloud tops of Jupiter seem to be divided into a series of bands that are different colors. The light bands are called zones, and the dark bands belts. The North Tropical Zone (equivalent to our northern temperate zone) is the brightest, its whiteness indicating high-level ammonia clouds. The Equatorial Belt, surrounding Jupiter's equator, always seems in turmoil, with the atmosphere constantly whipped up by violent winds. Across the planet are a number of white or red ovals. These are huge cloud systems. The brown and orange bands indicate the presence of organic molecules, including ethane.

Impact site

A MOMENTOUS IMPACT
In July 1994, fragments of the comet Shoemaker-Levy 9 crashed into Jupiter's southern hemisphere at speeds of around 130,500 mph (210,000 km/h). The comet had been discovered in 1993 by astronomers Carolyn and Eugene Shoemaker and David Levy, who also predicted its path. It was the first time in history that astronomers were able to predict a collision between two bodies in the Solar System and then observe the event. Over 20 pieces of the comet hit Jupiter, some of them sending up 1,865-mile- (3,000-km-) high fireballs and plumes.

Jupiter's moons

In 1610, Galileo (p. 20) made the first systematic study of the four largest moons of Jupiter. Since they seemed to change their positions relative to the planet every night, he concluded, correctly, that these objects must be revolving around Jupiter. This insight provided more ammunition for the dismantling of the geocentric theory (p. 11), which placed the Earth at the center of the Universe. In 1892 another small moon was discovered circling close to the cloud tops of the planet. Since then, over 55 more tiny moons have been discovered.

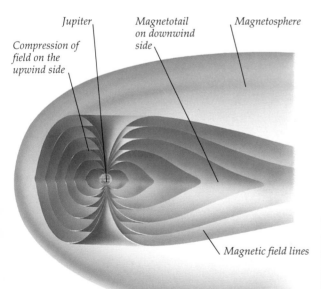

Compression of field on the upwind side

Jupiter

Magnetotail on downwind side

Magnetosphere

Magnetic field lines

SPINNING JUPITER
Jupiter spins so quickly that its day is only 9 hours and 55 minutes long and its equator bulges outward. Another effect of the rapid rotation is that the spinning of Jupiter's metallic hydrogen core generates a huge magnetic field around the planet. This magnetosphere is buffeted and pushed back by the solar wind and its tail spreads out over a vast distance, away from the Sun.

CALLISTO
Callisto is the second largest of Jupiter's moons, and the most heavily cratered, not unlike our Moon, except that the craters are made of ice. The bright areas are the ice craters formed by impacts of objects from space.

ERUPTION ON IO
Io is the Moon that is closest to Jupiter. It is one of the "Galilean" moons, named after Galileo, who discovered them. The others are Callisto, Europa, and Ganymede. The erupting plume of a massive volcano can be seen here on the horizon, throwing sulfuric materials 186 miles (300 km) out into space. The photograph was taken by *Voyager* from a distance of 310,700 miles (500,000 km) and has been specially colored using filters.

Saturn

THE GIANT PLANET SATURN, with its flat rings, is probably the most widely recognized astronomical image. For the classical world, Saturn was the most distant planet known. They named it after the original father of all the gods. Early astronomers noted its 29-year orbit and assumed that it moves sluggishly. Composed mostly of hydrogen, its atmosphere and structure are similar to Jupiter's, but its density is much lower. Saturn is so light that it could float on water (p. 45). Like Jupiter, Saturn rotates at great speed, causing its equator to bulge outward. Saturn also has an appreciable magnetic field. Winds in its upper atmosphere can travel at 1,100 mph (1,800 km/h) but major storms are rare. White spots tend to develop during Saturn's northern-hemisphere summer, which happens every 30 years or so, the last being in 1990.

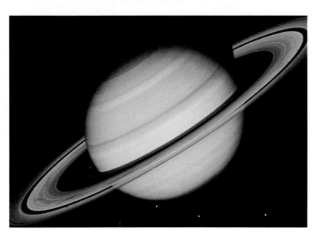

17TH-CENTURY VIEW
In 1675, the Bolognese director of the Paris Observatory, Gian Domenico Cassini (p. 28), discovered that, despite appearances, Saturn did not have a single, solid ring. He could see two rings, with a dark gap in between. His drawing, made in 1676, shows the gap, which was called the Cassini Division in his honor.

SATURN AND THE RINGS
Saturn's rings appear solid from the Earth, but the *Voyager* probes showed that they are composed of different-sized chunks of ice. The high reflectivity of these ice particles helps to explain Saturn's luminosity in the night sky. The rings themselves are only about 100 ft (30 m) thick, but the total width of the rings is more than 169,000 miles (272,000 km).

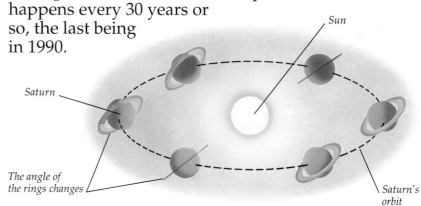

Sun

Saturn

The angle of the rings changes

Saturn's orbit

CHANGING VIEW
Saturn's axis is tilted. Because the rings lie around its equator, they incline as the planet tilts. This means that the rings change dramatically in appearance, depending on what time during Saturn's year they are being observed – Saturn's year is equal to 29.5 Earth years. The angle of the rings appears to change according to how Saturn and the Earth are placed in their respective orbits. When the rings are edge-on they look like a triple planet, as Galileo found in 1612.

Iapetus

Phoebe

Rings

Mimas

Tethys

Saturn

Enceladus

Titan

Hyperion

Calypso

MODEL OF SATURN
Planetaria and orreries are used to demonstrate the shapes and satellites of the planets. This orrery shows Saturn with the eight moons that were known in the 19th century. The model is flawed, however, because it is impossible to show the relative size of a planet and the orbits of its satellites.

SATURN'S WEATHER PATTERNS
The weather patterns of Saturn's northern hemisphere were photographed from a range of 4 million miles (7 million km) by *Voyager 2* in 1981. Storm clouds and white spots are visible features of Saturn's weather.

SEEING THE RINGS
When Galileo first discovered Saturn's rings in 1610, he misinterpreted what he saw. He thought Saturn was a triple planet. It was not until 1655 that the rings were successfully identified and described by the Dutch scientist and astronomer Christiaan Huygens (1629-1695), using a powerful telescope that he built himself.

Shadow cast by rings

Cassini's Division

Ring B

CLOSE-UP DETAIL
When Galileo studied Saturn in 1612, the two additional planets he thought he had seen in 1610 had disappeared. In 1616 they returned, flatter than before. What Galileo was seeing was Saturn's rings at different angles. Three sets of rings are visible from Earth. The "A" ring contains some of the orbits of the inner moons. The middle "B" ring is crossed by a series of lines that resemble the spokes of a wheel. Scientists think they may be dust particles suspended above the rings by the planet's magnetic field. In 1979 *Pioneer 11* discovered the bright, outer ring known as the "F" ring. At first glance, it seems braided, but further study shows that this plaiting is the result of a normal ring being pulled out of line by the gravity of nearby moons.

SATURN'S MOONS
All of Saturn's moons except the largest, Titan, are made of ice. Enceladus is a relatively small moon, and it shows evidence of recent change. Some parts of the moon are heavily cratered, while others are smooth, suggesting internal melting and subsequent surface melting. Enceladus has a diameter of 310 miles (500 km). This photograph was taken at a distance of 74,000 miles (119,000 km); features as small as 2 miles (3 km) can be identified.

Titan

Ring A

Rocky core

Liquid hydrogen

Metallic hydrogen

Atmosphere mainly hydrogen

Liquid hydrogen

FACTS ABOUT SATURN

- **Sidereal period** 29.4 Earth years
- **Temperature at cloud tops** –300°F (–180°C)
- **Rotational period** 10 hr 40 min
- **Mean distance from the Sun** 886 million miles/ 1.43 billion km
- **Volume** (Earth = 1) 744   • **Mass** (Earth = 1) 95.18
- **Density** (water = 1) 0.69
- **Equatorial diameter** 74,900 miles/120,535 km
- **Number of satellites** 31

Uranus

URANUS WAS THE FIRST PLANET to be discovered after the introduction of the telescope. It was discovered by accident, when William Herschel, observing from Bath, England, set about remeasuring all the major stars with his 6-in (15-cm) reflector telescope (p. 24). In 1781 he noticed an unusually bright object in the zodiacal constellation of Gemini. At first he assumed it was a nebula (pp. 60-61) and then a comet (pp. 58-59), but it moved in a peculiar way. The name of Uranus was suggested by German astronomer Johann Bode, who proposed that the planet be named after the father of Saturn, in line with established classical traditions. Bode is also famous as the creator of Bode's Law – a mathematical formula that predicted roughly where planets should lie.

WILLIAM HERSCHEL (1738-1822)
William Herschel was so impressed by a treatise on optics, which described the construction of telescopes, that he wanted to buy his own telescope. He found them too expensive, so in 1773 he decided to start building his own. From that moment on, astronomy became Herschel's passion.

North/south axis — Sun — Orbit

Ring — Direction of spin

ECCENTRIC TILT
Uranus spins on an axis that is tilted at an angle of nearly 98° from the plane of its orbit. This means that, compared with all the other planets in the Solar System, Uranus is spinning on its side. During its 84-year orbit of the Sun, the North Pole of Uranus will have 42 years of continuous, sunny summer, while the South Pole has the same length of sunless winter, before they swap seasons. This odd tilt may be the result of a catastrophic collision during the formation of the Solar System.

Ariel — Umbriel

Uranus

Titania

Oberon

19TH-CENTURY MODEL
Because of the odd angle of Uranus's rotational axis, all its known satellites also revolve at right angles to this axis, around Uranus's equator. This fact is demonstrated by an early model, which shows the planet and four of its moons tilted at 98°. The orrery (p. 36) dates from the 19th century, when only four of the 21 moons had been discovered.

VIEW FROM SPACE
Uranus is one of the great giant planets of the Solar System, four times larger than the Earth. All that can be seen is the tops of its clouds. Unlike Jupiter and Neptune, however, the clouds of Uranus are largely featureless. These two images show true color (left) and false color, photographed from 5.7 million miles (9 million km) away.

AIRBORNE OBSERVATION OF URANUS
The covering of one celestial body by another is known as occultation. A team of scientists observed the occultation of a star by Uranus in 1977 from NASA's Kuiper Airborne Observatory over the Indian Ocean. This was when the faint rings of Uranus were observed for the first time.

LITERARY MOONS
All the satellites of Uranus are named after sprites and spirits drawn from English literature. The American astronomer Gerard P. Kuiper (1905-1973) discovered Miranda in 1948. (Miranda and Ariel are characters from William Shakespeare's *The Tempest*.) It has a landscape unlike any other in the Solar System. Miranda seems to be composed of a jumble of large blocks. Scientists have suggested that these were caused by some huge impact during which Miranda was literally blown apart. The pieces drifted back together through gravitational attraction, forming this strange mixture of rock and ice.

URANUS RING SYSTEM
While watching the occultation of Uranus in 1977, astronomers noticed that the faint star "blinked on and off" several times at the beginning and end of the occultation. They concluded that Uranus must have a series of faint rings that caused the star to "blink" by blocking off its light as it passed behind them. The *Voyager 2* flyby in 1986 uncovered two more rings. The rings of Uranus are thin and dark, made up of particles only about 39 in (1 metre) across. The broad bands of dust between each ring suggest that the rings are slowly eroding.

THE MOON TITANIA
William Herschel discovered Uranus's two largest moons in 1789, naming them Oberon and Titania, the fairy king and queen in William Shakespeare's *A Midsummer Night's Dream*. English astronomer William Lassell (1799-1880) discovered Ariel and Umbriel in 1851. Miranda was discovered in 1948. Since then, a further 16 moons have been found.

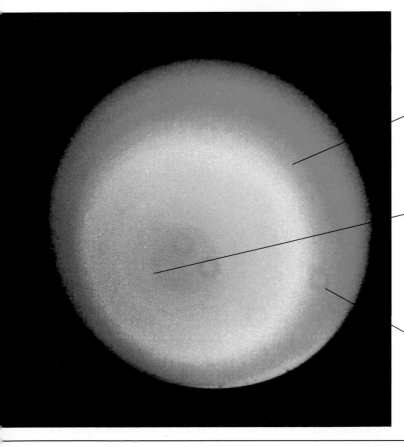

Color shows how haze affects the atmosphere

Polar region

Blemishes in processing

FACTS ABOUT URANUS

Hydrogen-rich atmosphere

Rocky core

Water, ammonia, and methane

- **Sidereal period** 83.8 Earth years
- **Temperature at cloud tops** – 350°F (–210°C)
- **Rotational period** 17 hr 14 min
- **Mean distance from the Sun** 1.785 billion miles / 2.87 billion km
- **Volume** (Earth = 1) 67
- **Mass** (Earth = 1) 14.5
- **Density** (water = 1) 1.29
- **Equatorial diameter** 31,765 miles / 51,120 km
- **Number of satellites** 21

Neptune and Pluto

NEPTUNE AND PLUTO WERE DISCOVERED as the result of calculations rather than observations – although, in the case of Pluto, these calculations were later found to be pure coincidence. By the early 19th century, astronomers realized that Uranus has a slightly irregular orbit because "something" is pulling it out of line. This is known as a "perturbation" – the gravitational pull of one body takes another off its expected course. In 1845 a young English astronomer, John Couch Adams (1819-1892), announced that he had calculated the probable position of another planet beyond Uranus, then located against the stars of Aquarius. His findings were ignored. In June 1846 another young astronomer, the Frenchman Le Verrier, published his findings about the extra-Uranian planet. Astronomers all over the world were asked to search for the new planet. On September 25, 1846 Johann Galle (1812-1910), astronomer at the Berlin Observatory, wrote to Le Verrier confirming the location of Neptune.

URBAIN LE VERRIER (1811-1877)
Le Verrier was a teacher in chemistry and astronomy at the *Ecole polytechnique*. Having calculated the position of Neptune, Le Verrier relied on others to do the actual "looking" for the planet for him.

NEPTUNE'S RINGS
Neptune, like all the giant planets, has a series of rings encircling it. The rings were discovered when the planet passed in front of a star. Results of an occultation (p. 55) in July 1984 showed the typical "blinking on and off," indicating that Neptune's rings were blocking out the light of the distant star. There seem to be two main rings, with two faint inner rings. The inner ring is less than 9 miles (15 km) wide. The rings were confirmed by *Voyager 2* in 1989.

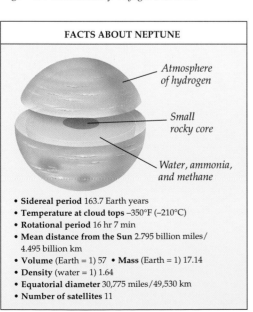

FACTS ABOUT NEPTUNE

Atmosphere of hydrogen

Small rocky core

Water, ammonia, and methane

- **Sidereal period** 163.7 Earth years
- **Temperature at cloud tops** –350°F (–210°C)
- **Rotational period** 16 hr 7 min
- **Mean distance from the Sun** 2.795 billion miles/ 4.495 billion km
- **Volume** (Earth = 1) 57 • **Mass** (Earth = 1) 17.14
- **Density** (water = 1) 1.64
- **Equatorial diameter** 30,775 miles/49,530 km
- **Number of satellites** 11

Great Dark Spot

Small clouds

Small clouds

Great Dark Spot

South polar region

NEPTUNE'S VANISHING GREAT DARK SPOT
In 1989 *Voyager* photographed a great storm system in Neptune's southern hemisphere. The storm, actually a hole in Neptune's upper cloud layer, was about the size of the Earth. Smaller clouds at the edges of the hole in this sequence – taken over a four-day period – suggested that the storm rotated counterclockwise. However, in the photographs taken of Neptune by Hubble in 1995, the storm had disappeared.

Discovering Pluto

In 1930, American astronomer Clyde Tombaugh (1906-1997) discovered the planet that lay beyond Neptune. It shifted very slowly against the background of the stars, showing that it was a long way away. An Oxford schoolgirl, Venetia Burney, suggested the name Pluto for the small, faint world, after the god of the underworld. Astronomers now know that Pluto is far too tiny to have any effect on Neptune's orbit. The calculations that led astronomers to look for Pluto were actually errors, and the discovery of the planet was due to Tombaugh's thorough work.

THE DISCOVERY OF TRITON

The moon Triton was discovered in 1846. It interests scientists for several reasons. It has a retrograde orbit around Neptune – that is, the moon moves in the opposite direction in which the planet rotates. It is also the coldest object in the Solar System with a temperature of –391°F (–235°C). Despite its low temperatures, Triton is a fascinating world. It has a pinkish surface, probably made of methane ice, which has repeatedly melted and refrozen. It has active geysers that spew nitrogen gas and darkened methane ice high into the thin atmosphere.

PERCIVAL LOWELL (1855-1916)

Lowell was born into a wealthy Boston family and was educated at Harvard. His interest in astronomy was stimulated by the reports of dark lines on Mars, and until his death he was a firm believer in intelligent life on Mars (p. 48). Later, Lowell became embroiled in a race to discover the planet beyond Neptune. Because he was looking for a planet that he believed was seven times heavier than the Earth, Lowell missed discovering Pluto, although the planet appeared on several of his photographs of the skies.

PLUTO AND CHARON

The distance between Pluto and its moon, Charon, is only 12,240 miles (19,700 km). Charon was discovered in 1978 by a study of images of Pluto that looked suspiciously elongated. The clear image on the right was taken by the Hubble telescope (p. 7), which allows better resolution than anything photographed from the Earth (left).

Sea-blue atmosphere

Ocean of water and gas

Smaller dark spot

CLOSE-UP OF NEPTUNE

This picture was taken by *Voyager 2* in 1989 after its 12-year voyage through the Solar System. It was 3.8 million miles (6 million km) away. *Voyager* went on to photograph the largest moon, Triton, and to reveal a further six moons orbiting the planet. Neptune has a beautiful, sea-blue atmosphere, composed mainly of hydrogen and a little helium and methane. This covers a huge internal ocean of warm water and gases – appropriate for a planet named after the god of the sea. (Many French astronomers had wanted the new planet to be named "Le Verrier," in honor of its discoverer.) *Voyager 2* discovered several storm systems on Neptune, as well as beautiful white clouds high in the atmosphere.

FACTS ABOUT PLUTO

Nitrogen-rich atmosphere

Large rocky core

Water ice

Water and methane ice

- **Sidereal period** 248 Earth years
- **Temperature** –375°F (–225°C)
- **Rotational period** 6 days 9 hr
- **Mean distance from the Sun** 3.65 billion miles/ 5.87 billion km
- **Volume** (Earth = 1) 0.006
- **Mass** (Earth = 1) .0022 • **Density** (Water = 1) 2.03
- **Equatorial diameter** 1,485 miles/2,390 km
- **Number of satellites** 1

Travelers in space

NOT ALL MATTER IN THE SOLAR SYSTEM has been brought together to form the Sun and the planets. Clumps of rock and ice travel through space, often in highly elliptical orbits that carry them toward the Sun from the far reaches of the Solar System. Comets are icy planetary bodies that take their name from the Greek description of them as *aster kometes*, or "long-haired stars." Asteroids are bits of rock that have never managed to come together as planets. Jupiter's powerful gravity flung the nearby debris into various eccentric orbits, causing some of the larger asteroids to crash together and break up. A meteor is a piece of space rock – usually a small piece of a comet – that enters the Earth's atmosphere. As it falls, it begins to burn up and produces spectacular fireworks. A meteor that survives long enough to hit the Earth – usually a stray fragment from the asteroid belt – is called a meteorite.

PREDICTING COMETS
Going through astronomical records in 1705, Edmond Halley (1656-1743) noticed that three similar descriptions of a comet had been recorded at intervals of 76 years. Halley used Newton's recently developed theories of gravity and planetary motion (p. 21) to deduce that these three comets might be the same one returning to the Earth at regular intervals, because it was traveling through the Solar System in an elliptical orbit (p. 13). He predicted that the comet would appear again in 1758, but he did not live to see the return of the comet that bears his name.

Comet's orbit

Sun

Comet's tail

COMET'S TAIL
Comets generally have elongated orbits. They can be seen by the light they reflect. As they get closer to the Sun's heat, their surface starts to evaporate and a huge tail of gas is given off. This tail always points away from the Sun because the dust and gas particles are pushed by solar wind and radiation pressure.

Nucleus

Erratic asteroid

Sun

Jupiter

Asteroid belt

Mars

KORONIS FAMILY OF ASTEROIDS
This photograph of the asteroid Ida was taken by the *Galileo* spacecraft in 1993 as the space probe traveled to Jupiter. The cratered surface probably resulted from collisions with smaller asteroids. Ida is 32 miles (52 km) long.

POSITION OF THE ASTEROID BELT
Since Sicilian monk Guiseppe Piazzi discovered the first asteroid in January 1801, nearly 10,000 asteroids have been found and named. Most of them travel in a belt between Mars and Jupiter, but Jupiter's great gravitational influence has caused some asteroids to swing out into erratic orbits.

KIRKWOOD GAPS
Measuring the distances of the known asteroids from the Sun in 1866, the American astronomer David Kirkwood (1814-1895) noticed that they tended to travel in loosely formed bands and that there were large, peculiar gaps between these bands. The gaps, which are now known as Kirkwood gaps, are due to recurring "bumps" from Jupiter's gravitational field. Asteroids can be catapulted into the inner Solar System by Jupiter's gravity.

Numbers of asteroids

Distance from Sun in astronomical units

When Halley's comet returned in
1986, the space probe *Giotto* was sent
out to intercept and study it. The
probe flew within 600 miles (960 km)
of the comet, took samples of the
vapor in its tail, and discovered
that its nucleus was a jagged
lump of dirt and ice
measuring 10 x 5 miles
(16 x 8 km).

Dust tail

Plasma (gas) tail

Meteorites

It was not until 1803 that the scientific community accepted that
meteorites did, indeed, fall from space. Over 95 percent of all
the meteorites recovered are stone meteorites. Meteorites are
divided into three types with names that describe the mix of
elements found within each specimen. Stony meteorites look
like stones but usually have a fused crust caused by intense
heating as the meteorite passes through the Earth's
atmosphere. Iron meteorites contain nickel iron crystals,
and stony iron meteorites are part stone, part iron.

MOLTEN DROPLET
Tektites are small, round, glassy
objects that are usually the size of
marbles. They are most often found
on the Earth in great numbers, all
together. When a blazing meteorite
hits a sandstone region, the heat
temporarily melts some of the
metals in the Earth's soil. These
molten droplets harden to form tektites.

Tektite

METEORITE IN AUSTRALIA
This meteorite (left) fell near the Murchison
River, Western Australia, in 1969. It contains
significant amounts of carbon and water. The
carbon comes from chemical reactions and not
from once-living organisms like those carbon
compounds found on the Earth, such as coal.

Geminids are seen in mid-December   *Perseids occur in mid-August*

*Quadrantids are seen
in early January*

Murchison
meteorite

METEOR SHOWERS
When the Earth's orbit cuts through a stream of meteors,
the meteoritic material seems to radiate out from one point
in the sky, creating a meteor shower. The showers are given
names, such as Geminid, that derive from the constellations
in the sky from which they seem to be coming.

Earth   *Sun*

ICY CRATER
The Earth bears many scars from large
meteorites, but the effects of erosion
and vegetation cover over some of the
spectacular craters. This space view
shows an ice-covered crater near
Quebec in Canada. It is now a
41-mile (66-km)-wide reservoir
used for hydroelectric power.

The birth and death of stars

Except for the Sun, the closest star to the Earth is Proxima Centauri, which is 4.2 light-years or 25 million million miles (40 million million km) away. A light-year is the distance that light or other electromagnetic radiation (p. 32) travels in a year. Stars are luminous, gaseous bodies that generate energy by means of nuclear fusion in their cores (pp. 38-39). As a star ages, it uses up its fuel. The core shrinks under its own weight while the nuclear "burning" continues. The shrinkage heats up the core, making the outer layers of the star expand and cool. The star becomes a "red giant." The more massive stars will continue to fuse all their lighter elements until they reach iron. As the remains of the star's atmosphere escape, they leave the core exposed as a "white dwarf." When a star tries to fuse iron, there is a massive explosion and the star becomes a "supernova." After the explosion, the star's core may survive as a pulsar or a "black hole" (p. 62).

CATALOG OF STARS
The French astronomer Charles Messier (1730-1817) produced a catalog of around 100 of the brightest nebulae (clouds of dust and gas) in 1784. Each object was numbered and given an "M-" prefix. For example, the Orion nebula is the 42nd object in Messier's list. Astronomers usually refer to this nebula as M42.

Venus — −4

0

Pole star — 1

Faintest star visible to the naked eye

Faintest star visible by optical telescope

HENRIETTA LEAVITT (1868-1921)
In 1912 the American astronomer Henrietta Leavitt was studying Cepheid variable stars. These are a large group of bright yellow giant and supergiant stars named after their prototype in the constellation of Cepheus. Variable stars are stars that do not have fixed brightness. Leavitt discovered that the brighter stars had longer periods of light variation. This variation can be used to determine stellar distances beyond 100 light-years.

Distant stars

Star in January

Parallax angle

Earth in July

Sun

Star in July

Parallax shift

Nearby star

Earth in January

CALCULATING DISTANCE
As the Earth orbits the Sun, stars that are closer to the Earth will seem to shift their location in relation to the background of more distant stars. This effect is called parallax, and it is used to calculate a star's distance from the Earth. The shift is measured in terms of an angle across the sky. This method is only accurate for stars within a few hundred light-years of the Earth. To show the effect, the illustration is not to scale.

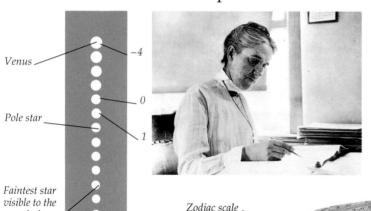

Zodiac scale

Month scale

Pole Star

Area of sky visible to viewer

Rule

STAR MAGNITUDES
A star is measured in terms of its brightness and its temperature. There is a difference between the apparent magnitude of a star – how bright it looks from the Earth, where we are looking over great distances – and its absolute magnitude, which is a measure of its real brightness. The scientific scale for apparent magnitude is based on ratios. Magnitude 1 is defined as being 100 times brighter than Magnitude 5. In this scale, the punched holes show the brightest star at the top and the faintest at the bottom.

A MAP OF THE STARS
Since ancient times, astronomers have had difficulties in being able to translate what is essentially a three-dimensional science into the medium of two dimensions. One solution was the planisphere, or "flattened sphere," in which the whole of the heavens was flattened out with the Pole Star at the center of the chart.

STUDYING THE STARS

British astronomer Williams Huggins (1824-1910) was one of the first to use spectroscopy for astronomical purposes (pp. 30-31). He was also the first astronomer to connect the Doppler effect (which relates to how sound travels) with stellar red shift (p. 23). In 1868 he noticed that the spectrum of the bright star Sirius has a slight shift toward the red end of the spectrum. Although his measurement proved spurious, he correctly deduced that this effect is due to that star's traveling away from the Earth.

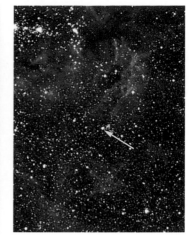

BETELGEUSE

Betelgeuse is a variable star that is 17,000 times brighter than our Sun. It lies on the shoulder of Orion the Hunter, 400 light-years from the Earth. Astronomers believe that it will "die" in a supernova explosion (above right).

NOVAE AND SUPERNOVAE

A nova was originally believed to be a newborn star. It is now known that novae are not new stars, but close double stars that flare up as one star loads its matter on to another. A supernova is much more violent, and takes place when a massive star collapses at the end of its life. Its core may, however, survive to become a small pulsating star (pulsar), or even a black hole. The gas blown off by the explosion forms an expanding shell. The gas from the supernova triggers the birth of new stars. These pictures show the appearance before (left) and after (right) of supernova 1987A over two weeks in 1987.

Outline of Orion, the Hunter

Bellatrix

THE STELLAR NURSERY

The material in a nebula – a stellar nursery made up of gases and dust – collapses under gravity and eventually creates a cluster of young stars. Each star develops a powerful wind, which clears the area to reveal the star surrounded by a swirling disc of dust and gas. This may form a system of planets or blow away into space.

Rigel

THE CONSTELLATION ORION

A constellation is a group of stars that appear to be close to each other in the sky, but that are usually spread out in three-dimensional space. Orion the Hunter's stars include the bright Betelgeuse and Rigel.

ORION NEBULA M42

Stars have a definite life cycle that begins in a mass of gas that turns into stars. This "nebula" glows with color because of the cluster of hot, young stars within it. This is part of the Great Nebula in Orion.

Our galaxy and beyond

THE FIRST GALAXIES WERE FORMED a few hundred million years after the Universe was born. As it contracted under its own gravity, each galaxy took on a certain shape. A typical galaxy contains about 100 billion stars and is around 100,000 light-years in diameter. Edwin Hubble was the first astronomer to study these distant star systems systematically. While observing the Andromeda Galaxy in 1923, he was able to measure the brightness of some of the stars in it, although his first estimate of their distance was incorrect. After studying the different red shifts of the galaxies (p. 23), Hubble proposed that the galaxies are moving away from our galaxy at speeds proportional to their distances from us. His law shows that the Universe is expanding.

EDWIN HUBBLE (1889-1953)
In 1923 American astronomer Edwin Hubble studied the outer regions of what appeared to be a nebula (p. 61) in the constellation of Andromeda. With the high-powered 100-in (254-cm) telescope at Mount Wilson, he was able to see that the "nebulous" part of the body was composed of stars, some of which were bright, variable stars called Cepheids (pp. 60-61). Hubble realized that for these intrinsically bright stars to appear so dim, they must be extremely far away from the Earth. His research helped astronomers to begin to understand the immense size of the Universe.

THE MILKY WAY
From the Earth, the Milky Way appears particularly dense near the constellation of Sagittarius because this is the direction of the galaxy's center. Although optical telescopes cannot penetrate the galactic center because there is too much interstellar dust in the way, radio and infrared telescopes can.

Elliptical galaxy

Spiral galaxy

Barred spiral galaxy

CLASSIFYING GALAXIES
Hubble devised a classification of galaxies according to shape. Elliptical galaxies were subdivided by how flat they appeared. He classified spiral and barred spiral galaxies (where the arms spring from a central bar) according to the tightness of their arms.

The Milky Way photographed from Chile with a wide-angle lens

Observatory building

WHIRLPOOL GALAXY
The Whirlpool Galaxy is a typical spiral galaxy, approximately 25 million light-years away. It can be found among the faint group of stars, Canes Venatici, at the end of the tail of the constellation of Ursa Major, or the Great Bear. It was one of the nebulae drawn by Lord Rosse (p. 26) in the 19th century.

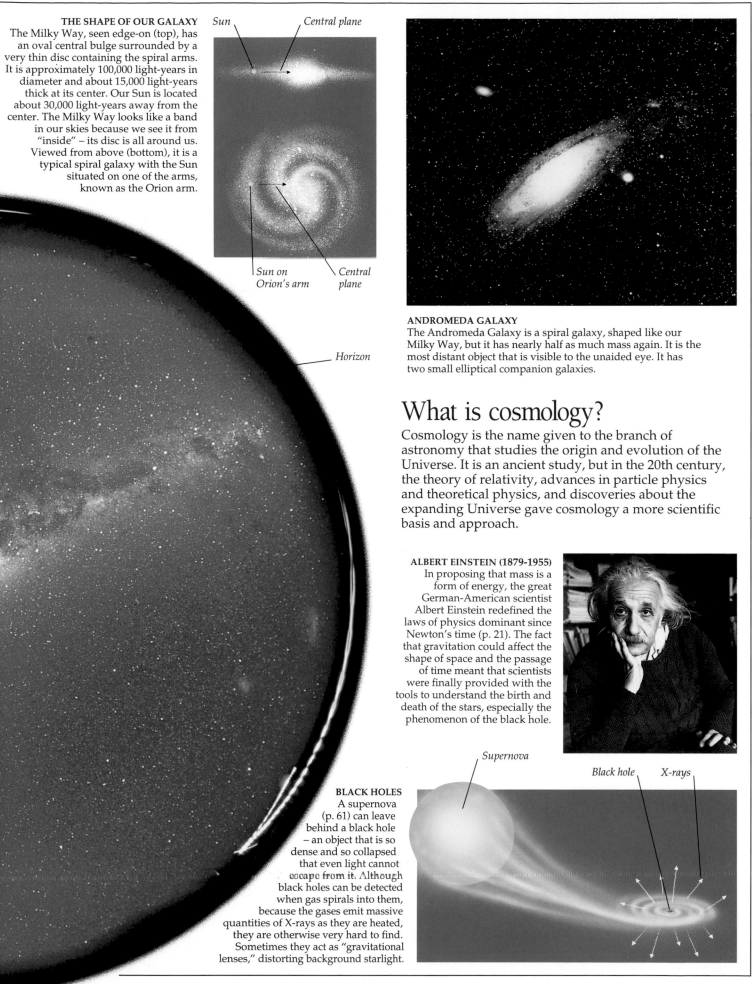

THE SHAPE OF OUR GALAXY
The Milky Way, seen edge-on (top), has an oval central bulge surrounded by a very thin disc containing the spiral arms. It is approximately 100,000 light-years in diameter and about 15,000 light-years thick at its center. Our Sun is located about 30,000 light-years away from the center. The Milky Way looks like a band in our skies because we see it from "inside" – its disc is all around us. Viewed from above (bottom), it is a typical spiral galaxy with the Sun situated on one of the arms, known as the Orion arm.

Sun

Central plane

Sun on Orion's arm

Central plane

Horizon

ANDROMEDA GALAXY
The Andromeda Galaxy is a spiral galaxy, shaped like our Milky Way, but it has nearly half as much mass again. It is the most distant object that is visible to the unaided eye. It has two small elliptical companion galaxies.

What is cosmology?

Cosmology is the name given to the branch of astronomy that studies the origin and evolution of the Universe. It is an ancient study, but in the 20th century, the theory of relativity, advances in particle physics and theoretical physics, and discoveries about the expanding Universe gave cosmology a more scientific basis and approach.

ALBERT EINSTEIN (1879-1955)
In proposing that mass is a form of energy, the great German-American scientist Albert Einstein redefined the laws of physics dominant since Newton's time (p. 21). The fact that gravitation could affect the shape of space and the passage of time meant that scientists were finally provided with the tools to understand the birth and death of the stars, especially the phenomenon of the black hole.

Supernova

Black hole

X-rays

BLACK HOLES
A supernova (p. 61) can leave behind a black hole – an object that is so dense and so collapsed that even light cannot escape from it. Although black holes can be detected when gas spirals into them, because the gases emit massive quantities of X-rays as they are heated, they are otherwise very hard to find. Sometimes they act as "gravitational lenses," distorting background starlight.

Did you know?

AMAZING FACTS

The International Space Station

Designed to carry out invaluable research, work on the International Space Station (ISS) started in 1998. Due for completion by 2008, it is being built entirely in orbit, involving spacewalks by astronauts and the use of space robotics.

Astronomers have found a pair of binary stars (KPD1930+2752) that could produce the most enormous Type Ia supernova ever. The two stars, which are in the constellation of Cygnus, are on course to collide some time in the next 200 million years.

Some galaxies are cannibals—they consume other galaxies! Hubble has taken pictures of the Centaurus A galaxy. At its center is a black hole that is feeding on a neighboring galaxy.

The *Galileo* spacecraft has taken amazing photographs of the surface of Jupiter's moon, Europa. It is crisscrossed with spectacular streaks up to 1,865 miles (3,000 km) long.

A color-enhanced view of Europa's surface

In 2003, astronomers announced that they may have witnessed the birth of a black hole. They reported a gamma-ray burst—a star explosion even brighter than a supernova. This occurs when a star up to 15 times the mass of our Sun (a Wolf-Rayet star) explodes.

A Wolf-Rayet star in its final hours

The world's largest optical telescopes are the Keck Telescopes in Hawaii. Each one is the height of an eight-story house.

The twin Keck Telescopes on Mauna Kea, Hawaii

The *Pioneer 10* spacecraft, which was launched in 1972, is still transmitting signals back to Earth, although NASA stopped monitoring them in 1997. Now more than 7 billion miles (11 billion km) away, *Pioneer 10* should reach the stars in the constellation of Taurus in about two million years.

Space flight missions have brought back samples of rocks from the surface of the Moon. Some of these rocks are up to 4.5 billion years old—older than any rocks found on Earth.

The Large Magellanic Cloud is a galaxy that orbits the Milky Way. It contains a dazzling star cluster known as NGC 1818, which contains over 20,000 stars, some of which are only about a million years old.

In 2000, scientists identified the longest comet tail ever. Comet Hyakutake's core was about 5 miles (8 km) across—but its tail measured over 350 million miles (570 million km) long.

By far the farthest planet, Pluto was discovered in 1930. It was given its name as a result of a suggestion made by 11-year-old English schoolgirl Venetia Burney.

The four telescopes that make up the Very Large Telescope

An artist's impression of the Overwhelmingly Large Telescope

Q Which is the most powerful telescope on Earth today?

A The Very Large Telescope (VLT) in Chile is the world's most powerful telescope. It is actually made up of four huge reflecting telescopes, but they are able to work together as one giant telescope. There are around 150 computer-controlled "actuators" underneath each mirror. These actuators adjust the reflecting surface by fractions of a millimeter to keep images in perfect focus. Each telescope—and the building that houses it—rotates to compensate for the Earth's rotation.

Q How far can astronomers see?

A The most distant galaxies so far detected are about 13 billion light-years away. This means that they were formed only a few hundred million years after the Big Bang.

Record Breakers

☾ **USING A TELESCOPE**
The first astronomers to study the night sky through a telescope were Thomas Harriott (1560–1621) and Galileo Galilei (1564–1642).

☾ **LARGEST INFRARED TELESCOPE**
The mirror of the Hobby-Eberly Telescope (HET) on Mount Fowlkes in Texas, is 36 ft (11 m) across.

☾ **PLANET WITH THE MOST MOONS**
Jupiter's moons numbered more than 60 at the last count—but astronomers are still finding new ones.

☾ **HIGHEST VOLCANO**
At 86,600 ft (26,400 m) high, Olympus Mons on Mars is the highest volcano in our Solar System.

☾ **NEAREST NEBULA**
The nearest nebula to Earth is the Merope Nebula, 380 light-years away.

Q How big will telescopes be in the future?

A The Overwhelmingly Large Telescope (Owl) is planned to be built in the Atacama Desert, Chile, by the year 2007. Its main mirror, made up of hexagonal segments, will be over 330 ft (100 m) across. Owl's designers hope to make use of both active and adaptive optics to achieve the best possible resolution. Active optics adjust the mirror segments so they work as a single sheet of glass. Adaptive optics work by shining a powerful laser into the sky, then adjusting the mirrors to keep the laser sharply in focus. This lets the telescope correct for distortions caused by the atmosphere.

Q Is Hubble the only space telescope?

A Launched in 1990, Hubble was the first major observatory in space. Then, in 1999, the Chandra X-ray Observatory went into orbit. Like Hubble, it has sent back extraordinary images. In February 2003, Chandra observed radiation around the "black widow" pulsar B1957+20, which is devouring its companion star. Hubble and Chandra are the most impressive space telescopes, but many satellites have had astronomical equipment on board. The Compton Gamma Ray Observatory (1991–2000), for example, carried four instruments designed to detect high-energy gamma radiation. Other satellites have been able to send back images based on their detection of radio waves, ultraviolet, infrared, or X-rays.

Q How does space technology help us find our way on Earth?

A As well as helping us map the Universe, satellites are also improving our ability to navigate on Earth. The Global Positioning System (GPS) is a collection of 27 satellites that are orbiting the Earth—24 in action and 3 back-ups. Their orbits have been worked out so that at any time there are at least four of them visible from any point on the planet. The satellites constantly broadcast signals that indicate their position. These signals can be picked up by devices called GPS receivers. A receiver compares the information from the satellites in its line of sight. From this, it can work out its own latitude, longitude, and altitude—and so pinpoint its position on the globe. GPS technology has some amazing applications. It is already being used in cars. By linking a GPS receiver to a computer that stores data such as street maps, an in-car system can plot the best route to a particular location.

GPS car navigation system

Cutting-edge astronomy

FINDING OUT HOW THE UNIVERSE was born is one of astronomy's most exciting challenges. Modern telescopes are not yet so advanced to solve the problem completely, but they can provide enough information about the early Universe to rule out some theories. Recently, astronomers have been using instruments that are able to detect microwaves from the remotest reaches of space. This radiation tells them about events that happened at the very start of the Universe, giving a glimpse of the shape of the Universe when it was just a few hundred thousand years old.

Back-to-back dishes scan deep space.

Solar array shields telescope from Sun's heat.

Instrument cylinder houses the equipment.

INTERFEROMETER TELESCOPE
The Degree Angular Scale Interferometer (DASI) does not look like a conventional telescope. Its job is to measure the fine detail of background radiation. DASI is sited at the South Pole, Antarctica, where freezing temperatures keep the atmosphere free of water vapor, sharpening the view into space.

MICROWAVE ANISOTROPY PROBE
For a better picture of the Cosmic Microwave Background (CMB), NASA sent its Microwave Anisotropy Probe (MAP) to a point four times farther out from Earth than the Moon, on the opposite side from the Sun. From this position the probe can view the whole sky without interference, measuring background radiation with pinpoint accuracy, to create a new map of the young Universe.

BOOMERANG TELESCOPE
In 1998, a microwave telescope nicknamed Boomerang flew over Antarctica for ten days at an altitude of 121,000 ft (37,000 m). The picture it sent back of around three per cent of the sky showed regular patterns in the CMB. They appear to be shock waves traveling through the young Universe—perhaps even echoes of the Big Bang.

The telescope waits to be lifted into the upper atmosphere.

Giant weather balloon filled with helium to float at very high altitudes

HUBBLE PICTURE OF A QUASAR
The Hubble Space Telescope is exploring deep space to dig up clues about other mysterious objects such as this quasar (left). Quasars are so bright that the galaxies surrounding them are almost invisible—unless astronomers "blot out" the central light in order to see what is happening nearby.

A giant black hole may drive quasar activity.

NEUTRINOS
This bubble chamber shows the pattern left by a sub-atomic particle called a neutrino after a high-speed collision. Some scientists hope that the mystery of the missing "dark matter" in the Universe could be solved by finding a new kind of heavy neutrino.

BIG BANG

BIG BANG
The CMB map is a strong piece of evidence for the Big Bang theory. If the Universe was once extremely hot and dense, and then cooled and expanded, a point should be reached when radiation would separate from matter. The trace this would leave behind matches the CMB.

CMB MAP
This map of the sky is laid out like any map of a globe—it shows the view in all directions from Earth. The most exciting thing for astronomers is that it is not perfectly uniform, but has patterns that give us clues about the forces at work in the Universe around 13 billion years ago.

Dark areas are cooler by a tiny percentage.

Hot spots show where galaxies will form.

Cosmic Microwave Background as seen by the MAP probe

STEPHEN HAWKING
Cosmologist Stephen Hawking worked with Roger Penrose to show how Einstein's theories about space and time support the Big Bang idea. Hawking used similar calculations to predict that black holes should be found to emit radiation.

Find out more

IF YOU WANT TO KNOW MORE about astronomy, just look at the sky! Binoculars or telescopes help, but there are around 2,500 stars that are visible to the naked eye. Invest in a pocket-sized guide to the constellations, so that you can identify what you observe. You can find tips on what to look for on a particular night at astronomy Web sites, on television specials, and even in some newspapers. You can also fuel your stargazing hobby by visiting science museums, which have lots of displays on space science of the past and the future.

Without tent light, stars would appear even brighter and clearer.

ASTRONOMY ON TV
Television shows can be a good introduction to the night sky. *The Sky at Night* is the world's longest-running astronomy program. In 1959, its host, Patrick Moore, showed audiences the first pictures of the far side of the Moon.

TV astronomer Patrick Moore

VISITING A PLANETARIUM
At a planetarium, stunning footage of the cosmos from world-class telescopes is projected on to a domed screen above your head. The planetarium shown below is in Brittany, France.

VIEWING THE NIGHT SKY
Anyone can be a stargazer. Using a standard pair of binoculars, this amateur astronomer has a great view of the Milky Way. The stars above the tent are in the constellation Sagittarius.

A seamless screen makes viewers feel like they are really viewing the sky.

ALIEN LIFE?
Perhaps one day astronomers will find definite proof of alien life. In the meantime, there are plenty of movies about other life forms. Of course they are pure fiction, and "real" aliens would probably look nothing like the movie versions, but they are still fun to watch!

The alien stars of *Mars Attacks!* (1996)

WHITE NOISE
You can see traces of the Cosmic Microwave Background just by turning on your television! When it is tuned between channels, the "snow" you see is partly microwave radiation from space.

WAITING FOR AN ECLIPSE

Eclipses are amazing events, but be sure to protect your eyes from the Sun's dangerous rays if you are lucky enough to see one. In any year, there can be up to seven solar or lunar eclipses. Although solar eclipses are more common, they seem rarer because they are only ever visible in a narrow area.

THE GIBBOUS MOON

The Moon is the ideal starting point for the amateur astronomer. Over a month you can observe each of its phases. This Moon, superimposed onto a photograph of Vancouver, Canada, is gibbous—that is, more than half full.

Places to visit

AMERICAN MUSEUM OF NATURAL HISTORY, ROSE CENTER FOR EARTH AND SPACE, NEW YORK, NEW YORK
• Hayden Planetarium
• Interactive exhibits explaining the history and scale of the universe

KENNEDY SPACE AND ROCKET CENTER, CAPE CANAVERAL, FLORIDA
• U.S. Astronaut Hall of Fame
• Hands-on exhibits demonstrating what it's like to explore space
• Rockets and hardware used in space, as well as a piece of Mars
• Virtual-reality theaters

ADLER PLANETARIUM AND ASTRONOMY MUSEUM, CHICAGO, ILLINOIS
• Virtual-reality experiences of the Universe
• Historical astronomical instruments

SPACE CENTER HOUSTON, HOUSTON, TEXAS
• A lifesize space shuttle to explore
• Real spacesuits, including John Young's ejection suit
• Behind-the-scenes tours of NASA's Johnson Space Center

NATIONAL MARITIME MUSEUM AND ROYAL OBSERVATORY, GREENWICH, UK
• Over two million objects, including a vast collection of astronomical instruments

Bronze equatorial sundial

ADLER PLANETARIUM AND ASTRONOMY MUSEUM
Most science museums have galleries dedicated to astronomy, but there are also specialist museums. Chicago's Adler Astronomy Museum has multimedia exhibits and an impressive array of antique telescopes.

USEFUL WEB SITES

• An excellent introduction from NASA for amateur astronomers: **http://spacekids.hq.nasa.gov/**
• Up-to-the-minute tips on what to look for in the night sky from the expert astronomers at Jodrell Bank Observatory: **www.jb.man.ac.uk/public/nightsky.html**
• The web site of the England's largest amateur astronomy society: **www.popastro.com**
• A different astronomical picture to look at every day: **http://antwrp.gsfc.nasa.gov/apod/astropix.html**

Glossary

Aurora borealis

APHELION The point in a planet's orbit where it is farthest from the Sun

ASTEROID A chunk of planet material in the Solar System

ASTROLOGY The prediction of human characteristics or activities according to the motions of the stars and planets

ASTRONOMICAL UNIT (AU) The average distance between the Earth and the Sun—93 million miles (150 million km)

ASTRONOMY The scientific study of the stars, planets, and Universe as a whole

ASTROPHYSICIST Someone who studies the way stars work

ATMOSPHERE The layer of gases held around a planet by its gravity. Earth's atmosphere stretches 600 miles (1,000 km) into space.

ATOM Smallest part of an element, made up of subatomic particles, such as protons, electrons, and neutrons

Charge coupled device (CCD)

AURORA Colorful glow seen in the sky near the poles, when electrically charged solar particles hit gases in the atmosphere

AXIS Imaginary line through the center of a planet or star, around which it rotates

BIG BANG Huge explosion that created the Universe around 13 billion years ago

BLACK HOLE A collapsed object with such powerful gravity that nothing can escape it

CHARGE COUPLED DEVICE (CCD) Light-sensitive electronic device used for recording images in modern telescopes

COMET An object of ice and rock. When it nears the Sun, it has a glowing head of gas with tails of dust and gas.

CONCAVE Curving inward

CONSTELLATION The pattern that a group of stars seems to make in the sky

CONVEX Curving outward

CORONA The Sun's hot upper atmosphere

CORONAGRAPH A telescope used to observe the edge (corona) of the Sun

COSMIC BACKGROUND RADIATION (CBR) A faint radio signal left over from the Big Bang

COSMOS The Universe

DOPPLER EFFECT The change in a wave frequency when a source is moving toward or away from an observer

ECLIPSE When one celestial body casts a shadow on another. In a lunar eclipse, Earth's shadow falls on the Moon. In a solar eclipse, the Moon casts a shadow on Earth.

ECLIPTIC Imaginary line around the sky along which the Sun appears to move

ELECTROMAGNETIC RADIATION Waves of energy that travel through space at the speed of light

ELECTROMAGNETIC SPECTRUM The complete range of electromagnetic radiation.

EQUINOX Twice-yearly occasion when day and night are of equal length, falling on March 21 and September 23

FOCAL LENGTH The distance between a lens or mirror and the point where the light rays it collects are brought into focus

FOSSIL The naturally preserved remains of animals or plants, or evidence of them

FREQUENCY The number of waves of electromagnetic radiation that pass a point every second

GALAXY A body made up of millions of stars, gas, and dust, held together by gravity

A communications satellite in geostationary orbit

GAMMA RAY Electromagnetic radiation with a very short wavelength

GEOLOGIST Someone who studies rocks

GEOSTATIONARY ORBIT An orbit 22,295 miles (35,880 km) above the Equator, in which a satellite takes as long to orbit Earth as Earth takes to spin on its axis

GRAVITY Force of attraction between any objects with mass, such as the pull between the Earth and the Moon

INFRARED Type of electromagnetic radiation also known as heat radiation

LATITUDE Position to the north or south of the Equator, in degrees

LIBRATION A wobble in the Moon's rotation that allows observers to see slightly more than half its surface

M2-9 planetary nebula

LIGHT-YEAR The distance light travels in a year—around 5.9 million million miles (9.5 million million km)

LONGITUDE Position to the east or west of the Prime Meridian, in degrees

MASS A measure of the amount of matter in an object and how it is affected by gravity

MATTER Anything that has mass and occupies space

MERIDIAN An imaginary line linking the poles. The Prime Meridian marks 0 degrees.

METEOR The streak of light seen when comet dust burns up as it enters the Earth's atmosphere

METEORITE A fragment of space rock that has fallen on to a planet or moon

METEOROLOGICAL To do with weather

MICROWAVE The type of radio wave that has the shortest radio wavelengths

NEBULA A cloud of dust and gas in space

NEUTRINO A subatomic particle produced by nuclear fusion in stars or the Big Bang

Pulsar with magnetic field shown in purple

NEUTRON STAR A collapsed star left over after a supernova

NOVA A white dwarf star that suddenly flares up and shines about 1,000 times brighter than before, after receiving material from a companion star

NUCLEAR FUSION When the nuclei (centers) of atoms combine to create energy

OBSERVATORY A place where astronomers study space

OCCULTATION When one heavenly body passes before another, hiding it from view

OORT CLOUD Huge spherical comet cloud, about 1.6 light-years wide and surrounds the Sun and planets

ORBIT The path of one object around another more massive object in space

PARALLAX Shift in a nearby object's position against a more distant background when seen from two separate points, used to measure the distance of nearby stars

PAYLOAD Cargo carried by a space vehicle or an artificial satellite

PERIHELION The point in an object's orbit where it is closest to the Sun

PHASE Size of the illuminated part of a planet or moon seen from Earth

PHOTOSPHERE A star's visible surface, from which its light shines

PLANET Large globe of rock, liquid, or gas that orbits a star

PRISM A transparent block used to change the direction of a beam of light

PROMINENCE A huge arc of gas in the Sun's lower corona

PULSAR A spinning neutron star

QUASAR A distant active galaxy releasing lots of energy from a central small area

RADIO TELESCOPE Telescope that detects radio waves from objects in space

REFLECTING TELESCOPE Telescope that gathers light with a concave mirror

REFRACTING TELESCOPE Telescope that gathers light with a combination of lenses

SATELLITE Any object held in orbit around another object by its gravity, including moons and artificial satellites

SIDEREAL TIME Time measured by the stars rather than by the Sun

SOLAR SYSTEM Everything held by the Sun's gravity, including planets and comets

SOLSTICE Twice-yearly occasion when the Sun is farthest from the Equator, falling on June 21 and December 21

SPECTROSCOPY The study of the spectrum of a body that emits radiation

STAR A hot, massive, shining ball of gas that makes energy by nuclear fusion

SUBATOMIC PARTICLE Particle smaller than an atom, for example a proton, neutron, or electron

SUNSPOT A cool dark spot on the Sun's surface, created by the Sun's magnetic field

SUPERNOVA An enormous explosion, created when a supergiant star runs out of fuel, or when a white dwarf explodes

TIDE The regular rise and fall of the sea caused by the gravitational pull of the Sun and the Moon on the Earth

False-color image of the Sun, showing dark red sunspots

ULTRAVIOLET Electromagnetic radiation with a shorter wavelength than visible light

VACUUM A perfectly empty—or very nearly empty—space

WAVELENGTH Distance between the peaks or troughs in waves of radiation

X-RAY Electromagnetic radiation with a very short wavelength

ZODIAC The 12 constellations through which the Sun, Moon, and planets appear to move

Index

Acknowledgments

The publisher would like to thank:
Maria Blyzinsky for her invaluable assistance in helping with the objects at the Royal Observatory, Greenwich; Peter Robinson and Artemi Kyriacou for modeling; Peter Griffiths for making the models; Jack Challoner for advice; Frances Halpin for assistance with the laboratory experiments; Paul Lamb, Helen Diplock, and Neville Graham for helping with the design of the book; Anthony Wilson for reading the text; Harris City technology College and The Royal Russell School for the loan of laboratory equipment; the Colour Company and the Roger Morris Partnership for retouching work; lenses supplied by Carl Lingard Telescopes, 89 Falcon Crescent, Clifton, Swinton, Manchester.

Illustrations Janos Marffy, Nick Hall, John Woodcock, and Eugene Fleury
Photography Colin Keates, Harry Taylor, Christi Graham, Chas Howson, James Stevenson, and Dave King.
Index Jane Parker

Picture credits
t=top b=bottom c=center l=left r=right

American Institute of Physics: Emilio Segrè Visual Archives/Bell Telephone Laboratories 32cl; W. F. Meggers Collection

32tl; Research Corporation 32bl; Shapley Collection 60cl; **Ancient Art and Architecture Collection:** 9tl, 9cr, 20tl; **Anglo-Australian Telescope Board:** D. Malin 61tr; **Archive für Kunst und Geschichte, Berlin:** 19tl; National Maritime Museum 46c; **Associated Press:** 8tl; **The Bridgeman Art Library:** 28tl; Lambeth Palace Library, London 17tr; **The Observatories of the Carnegie Institution of Washington:** 39cr; **Jean-Loup Charmet:** 60tl; **Bruce Coleman Ltd:** 43c; **Corbis:** Russeil Christophe/Kipa 69tl; Sandy Felsenthal 69r; Hulton-Deitsch Collection 68tl; **ET Archive:** 9tr; **European Southern Observatory:** 65tr; **Mary Evans Picture Library:** 6tl, 14bl, 18cb, 42tl, 61tcl; **Galaxy Picture Library:** Boomerang Team 66b; JPL 64bl; MSSS 49tr, 49br; Margaret Penston 67br; Robin Scagell 68bc; STScI 67tl; University of Chicago 66cl; Richard Wainscoat 27tl, 64br; **Gemini Observatory:** Neelon Crawford/Polar Fine Arts/US National Science Foundation 25cl; **Ronald Grant Archive:** 68cl; **Robert Harding:** R. Frerck 32bc; C. Rennie 10br; **Hulton Deutsch:** 20c; **Henry E. Huntington Library and Art Gallery** 62tl; **Images Colour Library** 7tl, 7tr, 7c, 16tl, 16cl, 18cl; **Image Select** 19br, 21tc, 23tl, 26cl, 28cr; **JPL** 3cr, 37cr, 44bl, 48br, 49c, 49cr, 50tr, 51crb, 52cl, 52br, 53cl, 55tr,

56cl, 63tr; **Lowell Observatory** 48tr; **Magnum:** E. Lessing 19tr; **NASA:** 3cr, 8cl, 35cr, 35bl, 38-39bc, 41cr, 44cl, 46br, 47b, 54-55bc, 56-57bc, 57tl; Dana Berry/Sky Works Digital 64c; JPL 34bc, 39tc, 49tl, 50br, 51bc, 53r, 55c, 55cr, 56cb, 61cr; WMAP Science Team 66tr; **National Geophysical Data Centre:** NOAA 27cl; **National Maritime Museum Picture Library:** 6cl, 10cr, 15tl, 15tr, 25tl, 27br, 29tr, 39c, 54tl; **Novosti (London):** 28br, 35cl, 47tr; **Planétarium de Brétagne:** 68-69; **Popperfoto:** 47tl; 67crb; **Rex Features Ltd:** 34clb; **Scala/Biblioteca Nationale:** 20cr; **Science Photo Library:** 18tl, 25bc, 31tl, 31bl, 48c, 53tl, 56tl, 57cr; Dr. J. Burgess 26tl; Chris Butler 70-71 bckgrd, 71br; Cern 67tr; Jean-Loup Charmet 11tl, 37tl; J-C Cuillandre/Canada-France-Hawaii telescope 68-69 bckgrd; F. Espenak 46tr; European Space Agency 35tl, 42-43bc; GE Astrospace 70cr; Jodrell Bank 33tr; Mehau Kulyk 67c; Dr. M. J. Ledlow 33tl; Chris Madeley 70tl; F. D. Miller 31c; NASA 7crb, 20bc, 20bcr, 20br, 34cr, 41crb, 44-45bc, 49tc, 51tr, 57cr, 58bl, 59br, 64t, 66-67 bckgrd, 67bc; NOAO 61cl, 71cr; Novosti 47cr; David Nunuk 25br, 65tl, 69tc; David Parker 70bl; Physics Dept. Imperial College 30crb, 30br; P. Plailly 38cl; Philippe Psaila 65br; Dr. M. Read 30tl; Royal Observatory, Edinburgh

59tr; J. Sandford 41t, 61bl; Space Telescope Science Institute/NASA 64-65 bckgrd, 71tl; Starlight/R. Ressemeyer 12tl, 27tr, 33cr, 55tl, 62-63c; U.S. Geological Survey 37br, 48l; Frank Zullo 68tr; **Tony Stone Images:** 42cl; **Roger Viollet/Boyes** 38tl; **Zefa UK:** 6-7bc, 8bl, 33b, 61br, 62bl; G. Heil 26bc.

With the exception of the items listed above, the object from the British Museum on page 8c, from the Science Museum on pages 21b, 22 cl, and from the Natural History Museum on page 43tl, the objects on pages 1, 2t, 2c, 2b, 3t, 3l, 3b, 3tr, 4, 11b, 12b, 14c, 14bc, 14r, 15tl, 15b, 16bl, 16br, 17tl, 17br, 20bl, 24bc, 25tr, 28cl, 28c, 28bl, 29tl, 29c, 29b, 31b, 36b, 38b, 40cl, 40bl, 40/4b, 42bl, 52bl, 54bl, 58tr, 60b, are all in the collection of the Royal Observatory, Greenwich.

Jacket images:
Front: Corbis/Digital Art (t); Charles O1Rear (b); DK Picture Library: National Maritime Museum (tr,tcr,tcrr).
Back: DK Picture Library: British Museum (tr); National Maritime Museum (cla, cr, crb, b).